# Trial & Error in Criminal Justice Reform
## Learning from Failure

Also of interest from the Urban Institute Press:

*But They All Come Back: Facing the Challenges of Prisoner Reentry,* by Jeremy Travis

*Juvenile Drug Courts and Teen Substance Abuse,* edited by John Roman and Jeffrey A. Butts

*Prisoners Once Removed: The Impact of Incarceration and Reentry on Children, Families, and Communities,* edited by Jeremy Travis and Michelle Waul

**THE URBAN INSTITUTE PRESS**
WASHINGTON, DC

# Trial & Error in Criminal Justice Reform

## Learning from Failure

### Revised Edition

Greg Berman
and
Aubrey Fox

THE URBAN INSTITUTE PRESS
2100 M Street, N.W.
Washington, D.C. 20037

**Library of Congress Cataloging-in-Publication Data**

The 2010 edition of this book was previously cataloged by the Library of Congress as follows:

Berman, Greg.
  Trial & error in criminal justice reform : learning from failure / Greg Berman and Aubrey Fox. p. cm.
    Includes bibliographical references and index.
    1. Criminal justice, Administration of—United States—Case studies. I. Fox, Aubrey.
  II. Title. III. Title: Trial and error in criminal justice reform.
  HV9950.B497 2010
  364.60973—dc22

                                                              2010017522

ISBN: 978-1-4422-6846-3 (cloth : alk. paper)
ISBN: 978-1-4422-6847-0 (pbk. : alk. paper)
ISBN: 978-1-4422-6848-7 (electronic)

Printed in the United States of America

12 11 10        1 2 3 4 5

**THE URBAN INSTITUTE** is a nonprofit, nonpartisan policy research and educational organization established in Washington, D.C., in 1968. Its staff investigates the social, economic, and governance problems confronting the nation and evaluates the public and private means to alleviate them. The Institute disseminates its research findings through publications, its web site, the media, seminars, and forums.

Through work that ranges from broad conceptual studies to administrative and technical assistance, Institute researchers contribute to the stock of knowledge available to guide decisionmaking in the public interest.

Conclusions or opinions expressed in Institute publications are those of the authors and do not necessarily reflect the views of officers or trustees of the Institute, advisory groups, or any organizations that provide financial support to the Institute.

# Contents

Acknowledgments | ix

Foreword | xiii

Introduction | 1

1 The Four Types of Failure | 11

2 Failure amid Success | 27

3 The Complicated Legacy of Operation Ceasefire | 45

4 The Billion-Dollar Failure: Parole and the Battle for Reform in California | 61

5 Beyond Simple Solutions:Mastering the Politics of Tragedy in Connecticut | 79

6 Defining Failure | 97

Conclusion | 113

Afterword                    125

Notes                        131

References                    137

Index                        143

About the Authors            149

# Acknowledgments

The origins of this book can be traced to a Greek restaurant in Hell's Kitchen on an unseasonably warm evening in the fall of 2005. At the table that night were Domingo Herraiz and Elizabeth Griffith from the U.S. Department of Justice's Bureau of Justice Assistance and Greg Berman and Julius Lang from the Center for Court Innovation. Much of the discussion was devoted to the subject of best practices in criminal justice. While everyone at the table agreed that it was important to identify and disseminate effective programs, there was also a consensus that the field of criminal justice was not particularly good at talking honestly about the reverse: projects that had failed to achieve their goals for one reason or another.

We didn't know it at the time, but that dinner conversation would ultimately spark a new initiative. Together, the Center for Court Innovation and the Bureau of Justice Assistance have spent the past several years studying failed criminal justice experiments and attempting to identify lessons for would-be innovators. This investigation, which is now led by Aubrey Fox of the Center for Court Innovation, has proven extraordinarily productive. Our partners at the U.S. Department of Justice deserve enormous credit for this. Our thanks to Laurie Robinson, Jim Burch, Drew Malloy, Betsi Griffith, Kim Norris, and Preeti Menon for their good humor and insight as well as their courage in supporting a project with the word "failure" in the title.

In attempting to put together a book on the subject of failure, we are fortunate to work for an organization, the Center for Court Innovation, that prizes both intellectual inquiry and the written word. These values were imprinted at the Center for Court Innovation by its founding director, John Feinblatt, who also helped spark our interest in criminal justice and sharpen our thinking about how to do good in the world. We owe him a great debt.

We also owe a debt to Mary McCormick, the president of the Fund for the City of New York, for her ongoing commitment to making the Center for Court Innovation run smoothly and for her friendship and sage counsel. These same qualities can be found among the leadership of the Center's other core institutional partner: the New York State Court System. Special thanks to Jonathan Lippman, Judith S. Kaye, and Ann Pfau for their faith in us over the years.

A number of our colleagues at the Center for Court Innovation have contributed moral, administrative, and intellectual support to this project, including Michael Rempel, Amanda Cissner, Sharon Bryant, Carol Fisler, Veronica Ramadan, Amy Levitt, Julius Lang, Robert Wolf, Alina Vogel, Don Farole, Liberty Aldrich, Valerie Raine, and Emily Gold. Special thanks to Adam Mansky, who shepherded the failure project during its early days, to Phil Bowen, who spent a year on loan with us from the British government, and to Alfred Siegel, who has done so much to help us hone our writing and reality-test our ideas.

During our research for this book, we have been inspired, both in print and in person, by a number of scholars and practitioners who have sought to advance a more forthright conversation about criminal justice reform. Among these are Joan Petersilia, Jeremy Travis, Eric Lane, Malcolm Feeley, David Kennedy, Lee Schorr, Michael Jacobson, Tony Thompson, Carol Weiss, Judy Harris Kluger, Anne Swern, Mindy Tarlow, Joel Copperman, Robin Steinberg, Mike Thompson, Geoff Mulgan, Tim Murray, Liz Glazer, Robert Keating, Gil Kerlikowske, Frank Hartmann, Herman Goldstein, George Kelling, Rick Rosenfeld, Michele Sviridoff, Michael Scott, Eric Lee, Herb Sturz, and Ron Corbett.

We also wish to thank all of those we interviewed for our case studies. Having seen our own work reflected in both the popular press and academic publications, we are sympathetic to how it feels to be on the other side of the fence. We are enormously grateful for the time and access we were given and have tried to honor that commitment by being evenhanded in our reporting and sensitive in our analysis.

The process of finding a publisher for a book on failure—no easy task even in the best of times and certainly nothing to take for granted in the current publishing environment—was aided and abetted by Malcolm Feeley of Berkeley Law School, Niko Pfund of Oxford University Press, and Candace McCoy of John Jay College. Thanks as well to David Shenk, Elizabeth Shreve, and Andy Postman for helping us learn the rules of the publishing game. We are grateful to have landed at the Urban Institute Press and the capable hands of Kathleen Courrier, Scott Forrey, and the rest of their team.

Finally, we wish to thank our families, who bore the brunt of supporting us through all of the ups and downs of writing a book while we simultaneously performed our day jobs.

For Greg, this includes Carolyn Vellenga Berman (who continues to set a high bar in terms of her commitment to her craft, her intellectual curiosity, and her ability to generate new ideas); Milly and Hannah Berman (whose talent and inventiveness as writers are a constant source of inspiration); and M. J. Berman, Allan Berman, and Michele Berman (who have provided living examples of the kind of grit and determination that are necessary to complete any significant task). I hope this book is some small recompense for the accommodations I have asked of all of you over the years.

For Aubrey, this book is dedicated to Robin Berg for her love, support, and good humor (not to mention editing skills), as well as to Robert Fox and Anita Sperling for encouraging a love of reading and writing from an early age.

# Foreword

*Cyrus R. Vance Jr.*

Academic researchers have long warned of the "file drawer effect": studies with successful results tend to be published, while failures get buried in file drawers. And so it is in criminal justice: successful programs are publicized and expanded. A statistically significant improvement in one jurisdiction is quickly extrapolated to herald the coming of a new millennium. And then, once the early promise proves to be overstated, programs are abandoned, and lessons forgotten.

The authors of this important and thoughtful book have combed through the file drawers of failed programs to draw lessons critical to anyone involved in criminal justice policy. While each program they study has at some point fallen short of expectations, there are enough genuine success stories along the way to encourage any of us who believe in innovation.

The lessons offered by this book are the same hard lessons taught by experience. No gain in the criminal justice system comes easily. In the real world, there is no guarantee that a thoughtfully designed program will even get off the ground. The best intentions are often met with skepticism by a community hardened by generations of broken promises.

Leadership, then, consists first in taking ownership of a program, committing to its success while not shrinking from the possibility of failure—and then engaging everyone with a stake in the outcome to join in that commitment.

Along with that must come honesty with ourselves and with our public. How often have you seen a report of a wonderful new rehabilitative program that boasts of only a 10 percent rate of recidivism? A recidivism rate that low means one of three things: either the program accepted only those participants who were already candidates for sainthood, the program stopped collecting recidivism statistics before the graduates removed their mortarboards, or recidivism was defined as only the most egregious violations of law.

Actually, there's a fourth possibility: maybe they made up the statistics altogether!

And so, another lesson of this book is that, from the outset, we must define success realistically. It is no doubt galling that despite the extraordinary efforts of reformers, some offenders refuse the offer of help, drop out at the first opportunity, or complete program requirements only to return to a life of offending. And it is every reformer's nightmare to see the tabloids treat a single recidivist as a case study in failure. That is why we must be clear from the outset that success will be defined as producing recidivism rates that are at least a little better, using public expenditures, than they were before.

Finally, this book warns us of that truism in criminal justice reform: even a successful program is difficult to replicate. But that does not mean that replication is impossible. It does mean that those who stand in the shoes of innovators must bring the same commitment and passion to replication as others did to invention. And it also means that the public should greet successful transplantation of programs from elsewhere with a level of enthusiasm comparable to that with which they greet home-grown success.

The lessons in this book are clearly drawn, but not always so easy to apply. In the office that I lead, we strive to innovate, and we strive equally to devise metrics by which we can measure success or failure. Today we run basketball programs in high-crime neighborhoods on Friday and Saturday nights; we support problem-solving courts for the addicted, the mentally ill, and victims of domestic abuse; we divert low-level offenders to youth court and counseling and keep their cases out of the criminal justice system altogether; and we pore over reams of crime statistics to understand the organization of gangs and posses and try to prevent violent crimes before they can be committed. We do so hopeful that we will meet with success, but with an equal commitment not to raise expectations unrealistically.

And while in all these endeavors we attempt to define the appropriate metrics and quantify results, we recognize that even the most intangible benefits deserve our dedicated efforts.

The philosopher John Dewey once wrote that understanding things the way they are is the first step in making them different. This book tells us that understanding failure is the first step to creating a fairer and safer community for everyone.

# Introduction

Men are greedy to publish the successes of [their] efforts, but meanly shy as to publishing the failures of men. Men are ruined by this one-sided practice of concealment of blunders and failures. (Burlingame 1997, 358)

—Abraham Lincoln

Name a social problem and chances are that someone has written a book about how to solve it. Interested in improving failing schools? Check out Wendy Kopp's *One Day, All Children: The Unlikely Triumph of Teach for America and What I Learned along the Way* (2003). Eradicating poverty? Try *Banker to the Poor: Micro-Lending and the Battle against World Poverty* by Muhammad Yunus (1999). Creating new jobs while saving the planet? There's *The Green Collar Economy: How One Solution Can Fix Our Two Biggest Problems* by Van Jones (2008). We could go on, but you get the picture. In general, the world of public policy is inundated with books about "best practices" and "evidence-based programs"—exemplary ideas and initiatives that offer the promise of guaranteed success.[1]

In truth, the world probably does not need another book that markets success. But failure . . . well, that's a different story. Failure is typically discussed only in hushed whispers in the world of civic affairs.

In his effort to usher in "a new era of responsibility," President Barack Obama has demonstrated a refreshing candor about his own mistakes. But this is still the exception and not the rule in public policy. Fear of failure is, of course, part of human nature. And experience tells us that the instinct for self-preservation can kick into overdrive when careers, reputations, and dollars are on the line. The higher the stakes, the less likely you are to hear the "F word."

But there are real consequences when we fail to talk about failure. Most obviously, it leads to an environment that stifles innovation. Without a willingness to try new ideas and risk failure, it is impossible to imagine how we are ever going to challenge conventional wisdom or address our most difficult social problems.

Unfortunately, the field of criminal justice has been particularly slow in embracing the value of trial and error. In other disciplines, most notably science and medicine, solving problems is viewed as an iterative process.[2] There is an old quote, attributed to Thomas Edison, that neatly encapsulates the importance of the scientific method: "I have not failed 5,000 times. I have successfully discovered 5,000 ways that do not work and I do not need to try them again." More recently, Eli Lilly & Company's chief science officer was renowned for holding "failure parties" as a way of acknowledging outstanding scientific work even if it ultimately failed to lead to new drugs for the company.[3]

Needless to say, there are no failure parties in criminal justice. Criminal justice officials are rarely afforded the opportunity to engage in a trial-and-error process, partly because the consequences of failure are so immediate (people can die) and partly because the media and political environment that surround the crime issue will not let them (people get fired). Is it any wonder that a "cover your ass" mentality dominates many criminal justice agencies? Policing expert and University of Wisconsin Law School Professor Michael Scott describes the problem this way: "Very seldom do police chiefs say, 'We had a great idea that didn't work. We're going back to the drawing board to do it differently.' That's what a scientist would say without batting an eye, but a police chief often doesn't feel that he or she has that kind of latitude" (Scott 2008).

To be fair, it is not accurate to say that there is no discussion whatsoever about failure in the criminal justice system. There are, in fact, built-in mechanisms for dealing with certain kinds of failures—most notably, civilian complaint review boards and the appellate review process. Partially because of these kinds of institutions, public discussion about the shortcomings of the criminal justice system tends to focus on such hot-button issues as police misconduct and the death penalty. As important as these topics may be morally and philosophically, they involve very few people and have only a marginal impact on public safety. They also offer few meaningful lessons for policymakers and would-be innovators.

Learning lessons from the past is not a particular strength of the criminal justice system. Indeed, the history of criminal justice in the United

States can be read as a swinging pendulum, as policymakers have veered from punitiveness to leniency and back again, without pausing to remember why they initially favored one approach over the other. The reluctance of criminal justice policymakers to talk openly about failure has helped fuel this dynamic. It has stunted the public conversation about crime in this country and stifled new ideas. It has also contributed to our inability to address such problems as chronic offending in low-income neighborhoods, an overreliance on incarceration, the misuse of pretrial detention, and the high rates of recidivism among parolees. Unless criminal justice policymakers and practitioners are given the time, space, and encouragement to learn from their predecessors and analyze their own foibles, the field will forever find itself haunted by Georges Satayana's dictum that "those who cannot remember the past are condemned to repeat it."

We have chosen to write a book on failure in the criminal justice system in an effort to escape this fate. Our goal is to encourage a more forthright dialogue about criminal justice, one that acknowledges that many new initiatives fail and that no one knows for certain how to reduce crime. For us, this is not a source of pessimism but a call to action. By openly discussing and even celebrating failure, we seek to help foster a climate that encourages the development and implementation of new ideas based on rigorous reflection.

To be clear, when we use the term "failure," we do not mean errors of incompetence or corruption—the judge who mistakenly rules a crucial piece of evidence inadmissible or the police officer who is on the payroll of local drug dealers. Nor are we focused on the kinds of societal failures—poverty, racism, the breakdown of the American family—that are so often intertwined with the criminal justice system.

Rather, this book is devoted to examining well-intended efforts that for one reason or another fell short of their stated objectives. These efforts include high-profile national programs, such as the Drug Abuse Resistance Education (D.A.R.E.) program, which has sent thousands of police officers into local schools to educate students about drugs without making a dent in teen substance abuse. We also look at lesser-known local initiatives, such as the St. Louis police department's creative, but ultimately flawed, program to reduce gun violence by asking the worried parents and guardians of teenagers for permission to inspect their homes for firearms in return for a promise not to make any arrests based on what they found.

By design, we examine several initiatives that have been widely hailed as successes, including drug courts (which link addicted offenders to drug treatment in lieu of incarceration) and Operation Ceasefire (a strategy to send a more coherent message of deterrence to individuals who are responsible for the lion's share of violence in a given jurisdiction). While drug courts and Operation Ceasefire have achieved impressive results in many places, in some locations they have struggled to succeed. Our implicit message in looking for failure amid success is that the line between the two is not as clear as some may think.

In writing this book, we drew upon three years' worth of research into the failed criminal justice experiments of the past. This research, which was underwritten by the U.S. Department of Justice's Bureau of Justice Assistance, included a literature review, roundtables, on-site observations of innovative projects, and interviews with dozens of leading practitioners and scholars in the field.

This research has been buttressed by our own life experience. For the past decade, we have worked at the Center for Court Innovation, a not-for-profit organization that seeks to help the justice system reduce crime, aid victims, and promote public trust in justice. The Center for Court Innovation has won national prizes for innovation from the Drucker Institute, American Bar Association, National Criminal Justice Association, National Association for Court Management, Ford Foundation, and Harvard University's John F. Kennedy School of Government.

In particular, the Center has been honored for its success in conceiving, planning, and implementing model projects that seek to focus the energies of the justice system on addressing the problems of addiction, mental illness, domestic violence, and quality-of-life crime. These "problem-solving courts" include two projects that the two of us served as lead planners for: the Red Hook Community Justice Center and Bronx Community Solutions.

The Red Hook Community Justice Center is a community court located in a Brooklyn neighborhood that has long been notorious for drugs, crime, and disorder. In response, the Justice Center—a joint project of the Center for Court Innovation, the New York State Unified Court System, the City of New York, the Kings County District Attorney's Office, and others—has sought to reduce fear and improve public safety.

Operating out of a refurbished Catholic school that previously had been vacant for decades, the Justice Center is home to a multifaceted courtroom, presided over by the Hon. Alex Calabrese, that handles minor criminal matters, landlord-tenant disputes, and juvenile delinquency cases. Whenever possible, the Justice Center seeks to link defendants and litigants to social services, including drug treatment, job training, and mental health counseling, with the goal of helping them avoid a return to court. At the same time, the Justice Center serves as a launching pad for an array of crime prevention and community engagement initiatives, including but not limited to a youth court, youth baseball league, police-teen theater workshop, and an AmeriCorps community service program.

The Justice Center's novel approach to justice has contributed to the transformation of what was once a dreary neighborhood. Crime is down, investment in the community is up, and researchers have documented improved attitudes toward government.

In 2005, we brought some of the ideas piloted by the Red Hook Community Justice Center to the Bronx, but with a twist. Instead of working in a single neighborhood with just one judge, we have attempted to go to scale with problem-solving justice by providing the four dozen judges who handle misdemeanor criminal cases in the Bronx, a borough of 1.4 million people, with the same kind of sentencing options that Judge Calabrese in Red Hook utilizes.

Our goal in the Bronx is a simple one: to make justice in low-level cases more meaningful. While this experiment is still relatively young, there are encouraging results to report. The project already has changed sentencing practice in the Bronx—in thousands of cases, the use of short-term jail has been replaced by community restitution and social services. Bronx Community Solutions also has won considerable neighborhood support by contributing tens of thousands of community service hours to the Bronx each year, putting minor offenders to work sweeping the streets, painting over graffiti, and cleaning local parks.

Both the Red Hook Community Justice Center and Bronx Community Solutions have been hailed as national models. Each year, these projects are visited by hundreds of criminal justice officials from across the country and around the world. Replications have been spawned in places both near (New Jersey and Connecticut) and far (Canada, Australia, and England).

As gratifying as this attention has been, we know that every success that the Red Hook Community Justice Center and Bronx Community Solutions have experienced has been the result of a laborious trial-and-error process that inevitably involves disappointment along the way. We have had a role in creating technology applications that frustrated end users, mentoring programs that struggled to find mentors, antiviolence initiatives that proved impossible to sustain over time. . . . The list goes on and on.

In reflecting upon our failures as well as the failures of others, we have identified four principal themes that come up time and time again. These are the themes that animate this book.

1. *Not all failures are alike.* Failure is usually the product of a complicated chemistry involving a specific time, a specific place, and specific personalities. While every failure has its unique elements, failures generally fall into four distinct groups. The first two are relatively straightforward: failure of concept (a bad idea) and failure of implementation (poor execution). Sometimes, reformers just get it wrong, fundamentally misunderstanding the nature of the problem they are trying to address or failing to pay the necessary attention to service delivery. Two other kinds of failure are less obvious: failure of marketing and failure of self-reflection. These are essentially opposite sides of the same coin. On one hand, innovators will not get very far if they do not manage politics well or if they are incapable of winning the necessary resources to implement their ideas. On the other hand, some reformers become so intent on drumming up support that they fail to assess their own weaknesses or to respond quickly as facts on the ground change. In chapter 1, we use the Consent to Search program in St. Louis to highlight the various ways in which a criminal justice experiment can fail.

2. *Failure is rarely black and white.* While the press and politicians tend to want bottom-line answers ("Does this program work or not?"), the reality usually is more nuanced: some initiatives work for some people some of the time. Moreover, the definitions of success and failure often depend on where one stands—and what one values. This is particularly true in the criminal justice system, where the principal actors often have conflicting agendas. Michael Schrunk, the elected prosecutor in Portland, Oregon, offers this example: "If pretrial services succeeds in getting more people out of jail, they might define that as a success, whereas the local police force or prosecutor might not see that as being in their interest. . . . It is very difficult to get everybody at the table to agree on specific strategies because a lot of times they see it as, 'If you win, then I lose' " (Berman 2008). In our final chapter, we explore the difficulty of defining failure

in greater detail, through the prism of the controversy over the D.A.R.E. program.

3. *Politics plays an enormous role in the success or failure of any reform.* Most innovations require government support or endorsement at some level, so criminal justice reformers constantly must grapple with the political realities of elected officials and high-ranking bureaucrats. It is tempting, particularly for "good government" types, to portray reform initiatives as somehow rising above the political concerns that typically drive government decisionmaking. This is a recipe for disaster. But it is also true that, in order to mobilize political support and generate funding, reformers often find it necessary to overstate the potential impacts of their work. According to criminologist Joan Petersilia, when it comes to criminal justice reform, "there's a long history of over-promising and under-delivering":

> There is nothing in our history of over 100 years of reform that says that we know how to reduce recidivism by more than 15 or 20 percent. And to achieve those rather modest outcomes, you have to get everything right: the right staff, delivering the right program, at the right time in the offender's life, and in a supportive community environment. We just have to be more honest about that, and my sense is that we have not been publicly forth-coming because we've assumed that we would not win public support with modest results (Berman and Fox 2008, 24).

Petersilia is describing a common failure trap that reformers stumble into repeatedly. Unfortunately, failure is often as much a matter of perception as reality: even the best designed and implemented initiatives will be viewed as failures if reformers are not careful about managing expectations. The importance of politics—with both a big "P" and a small "p"—is woven throughout this book, most explicitly when we examine the checkered histories of drug courts in Minneapolis and Denver and tell the remarkable story of how officials in Connecticut were able to resist calls for "three strikes and you're out" legislation despite public outrage over one of the most shocking crimes in recent years.

4. *Implementation is as important as ideas.* Translating concepts into concrete programs is not easy. The truth is that the majority of new policy initiatives fail, just as the majority of new businesses fail. One of the most common obstacles is the challenge of context: what works in Los Angeles might not work in Chicago, let alone in a rural parish in Louisiana.

According to Lisbeth Schorr, professor at Harvard University, "Context is the most likely saboteur of innovations. The biggest mistake is thinking that because a program is wonderful, the surroundings won't destroy it when you plunk it down in a new place" (Berman and Fox 2002, 7). Or, as the singer Billy Bragg puts it, "You can borrow ideas, but you can't borrow situations."[4] Our chapter on the struggles of Operation Ceasefire to maintain and replicate its success in Boston in the 1990s illustrates this point. Reformers also must understand the importance of winning support from frontline workers (police officers, judges, prosecutors, parole officers). As difficult as it is to win battles among policy elites at the top levels of government, often the most important policy decisions are made at the ground level by "street-level bureaucrats" (Lipsky 1980). This lesson is underlined in our examination of the battle to reform parole in California.

In selecting our failure case studies, our goal was neither to assign blame nor to engage in the kinds of critiques that are only possible with the benefit of 20-20 hindsight—indeed, we came away from our research with renewed respect for all those with the courage to attempt to change an institution as vast and complex as the criminal justice system. Nor is our goal to send the message that change is impossible. Quite the contrary. We seek to foster criminal justice innovation by acknowledging the reality that failure, while not desirable, is often inevitable and even acceptable, if it is properly analyzed and used as a learning experience. Even initiatives that fall short of their goals can provide valuable information and guidance as we look to improve the criminal justice system in the future.

While this book is about failure, it is worth noting that in many respects we are living in a period of remarkable success for the American criminal justice system. During this time, historic crime drops have made citizens safer, reduced victimization, and pushed public safety from the top to the bottom of the public agenda. Numerous theories have been advanced to explain the crime reductions of the past 20 years. Some have focused on metatrends, such as changing birth rates, an economy that until recently was expanding, the decline of crack cocaine, and even fluctuations in abortion rates. Others have pointed to discrete criminal justice innovations, such as drug courts, sentencing reforms, the CompStat crime mapping and management system, and community and problem-oriented policing. No matter which explanation one favors, it is safe to say that the field of criminal justice has come a long way from the days of "nothing works" and "ungovernable cities."[5]

While there is much to be proud of, there is still more to be done. Despite significant advances in knowledge and practice over the past 20 years, American criminal justice agencies are still struggling to understand how to tackle problems like gangs, gun crime, and domestic violence. The system still relies on incarceration as a default setting, even in cases where it might be cheaper and more effective to use community-based alternatives. Roughly two-thirds of ex-offenders commit a new offense within three years of leaving prison. Probation and parole supervision are often empty rituals because underresourced officers are routinely asked to supervise dozens of offenders simultaneously. There is no shortage of problems still to be addressed.

Unless criminal justice officials are willing try new approaches and risk failure, we are unlikely to make a dent in these problems. According to Kevin Burke, a Hennepin County (Minnesota) trial court judge whom we will meet again in our chapter on drug courts, "We have to fight against the tendency to always choose a traditional approach to problems. A more common source of failure in criminal justice is an unwillingness to try anything different" (Berman and Fox 2008, 21).

The need for consistent and persistent risk taking was perhaps best communicated by a Nike commercial made at the height of Michael Jordan's career. In the spot, Jordan says, "I've missed more than 9,000 shots in my career. I've lost almost 300 games. Twenty-six times I've been trusted to take the game-winning shot . . . and missed. I've failed over and over and over again in my life. And that is why I succeed."[6]

In writing this book, we hope to encourage criminal justice reformers to fail over and over again so they will ultimately succeed.

# 1

# The Four Types of Failure

I t all started with a suggestion made by a frustrated mother at a community meeting in 1993. St. Louis was experiencing an epidemic of gun violence that was killing hundreds of young men and women. The mother wanted to know why the police would not search a nearby house that she thought was being used by teenagers to stash firearms. Told that her word alone was not legally sufficient to obtain a search warrant, she bluntly replied, "Why don't you just knock on the door and *ask* the mother if you can search the house?"

Lieutenant Joseph Richardson was struck by the woman's reasoning. After all, with the parent's permission, the police would be on solid legal grounds. "I could think of no logical reason why I couldn't ask to search," Richardson said.

At that moment, an innovative program designed to get guns out of the hands of teenagers was born, nursed into being by a small group of police officers and researchers. The idea was simple: the police would ask parents in high-crime areas if they could search their homes for firearms. To encourage the parents to agree, the police promised not to make any arrests if they found an illegal handgun, illegal drugs, or stolen goods. Sacrificing arrests to get guns off the streets was an unconventional strategy, but it seemed like a reasonable experiment in light of the violence plaguing St. Louis.

This initiative, which came to be called the St. Louis Consent to Search program, started brightly. Aggressive and committed officers took hundreds of guns off the street in the program's first 18 months. Results like these attracted national attention. President Bill Clinton even mentioned the program in one of his weekly radio addresses. Unfortunately, that was about as good as it got for the St. Louis Consent to Search program. By 1999, just six short years later, it was effectively dead.

Unfortunately, what happened in St. Louis is not unique. In criminal justice, as in any area of public policy, programmatic failures are common. That's the dirty little secret that very few policymakers or public officials are willing to admit openly. The truth is that many social innovations are destined to fail, not because practitioners are corrupt or incompetent (although corruption and incompetence do exist), but because meaningful change is exceedingly difficult to achieve.

What makes the St. Louis Consent to Search program different is that, unlike most run-of-the-mill failures, two criminologists from the University of St. Louis-Missouri, Richard Rosenfeld and Scott Decker, were thoughtful enough to write a detailed chronicle of the project's fits and starts for the National Institute of Justice. In other words, rather than disappearing without a trace, the St. Louis Consent to Search program left us a trail of clues to decipher and learn from.[1]

## A New Idea

The Consent to Search story begins as many policy innovations do: with a crisis. In the early 1990s, the murder rate in St. Louis was close to 70 per 100,000 residents, one of the top five rates in the nation. (At the time, the U.S. rate was about 8 per 100,000.) For black men age 15 to 19 in St. Louis, the murder rate was 380 per 100,000 citizens. Astonishingly, the rate was 600 per 100,000 black men in St. Louis age 20 to 24. Ninety-eight percent of the victims were killed by firearms.

St. Louis was a city under siege. The local newspaper printed a daily body count. A group of churches announced plans for a "murder-free month." Despite these efforts, homicides continued to rise.

Nothing seemed to be working to stem the tide of violence. One of the city's first prevention efforts was a massive gun buyback program that netted over 7,500 guns in 1991. A follow-up evaluation found that the program was almost completely ineffective as a crime-fighting tool. Precious few of the guns that were turned in came from the at-risk young people in St. Louis who were killing each other every day. But it gets worse. A disturbingly large share of the young people who did participate in the program told researchers that they planned to use the money they earned from the sale to buy better guns (Plotkin 1996). Gun buybacks were clearly not the answer to St. Louis's problems.

While everyone involved with criminal justice in St. Louis was under enormous pressure to reduce gun violence, the burden fell most heavily on the police. Within the St. Louis Police Department, the Mobile Reserve Unit had a reputation for attracting the city's toughest police officers. Housed in a nondescript warehouse miles from police headquarters, the Mobile Reserve Unit was given the freedom to respond to crime anywhere in the city as opposed to staying within the boundaries of a single precinct.

The Mobile Reserve Unit incubated the Consent to Search program. The aptly named Sergeant Simon Risk took the lead. Risk had a reputation as a smooth talker with an instinctive knack for putting people at ease. "He was not typical police," said his colleague Sergeant Bob Heimberger. "Simon could make anyone feel comfortable" (Heimberger 2008). While other officers would have scoffed at the idea of politely knocking on doors that they normally would have broken down with a battering ram, Risk was game to try.

The U.S. Supreme Court gives law enforcement officials wide latitude to search the property of juveniles with parental consent, but only if that consent is given freely. To help underscore the voluntary nature of the program, Risk developed a "consent to search and seize" form that would be carefully reviewed and signed by parents before the police went forward with a search. Among other things, the form specified that no arrests would be made by the officers if they found any illegal property, including guns or drugs, although such property was subject to seizure. Perhaps more importantly, the officers involved developed a low-key approach in working with parents. As one officer put it, "We don't go in like storm troopers. We realize that this concept makes groups like the ACLU leery, so we want to avoid complaints. Using a soft approach is why this program has worked. We don't intimidate anyone" (Decker and Rosenfeld 2001, 7). This approach paid off: as they hoped, the program attracted only faint criticism from civil libertarians.

Risk began by visiting the homes of young people previously arrested on firearm-possession charges. He and another officer, part of a small group of handpicked recruits, would approach a house, knock on the door, explain that they were concerned about the toll guns were taking on the city, and ask an adult for permission to conduct a search. Almost immediately the officers realized they were on to something. Not only were parents willing to let them search the house, they were often grateful that the police cared enough to try to help them. Many parents were terrified that their children were going to end up either in jail or dead. One woman who worked the night shift at a local hospital offered to give the police her key so that they could search the house anytime they wanted. Another woman asked if she could sign a stack of predated forms.

Before long, the majority of referrals for consent searches came from community members who had heard about the program, instead of from internal police referrals. This greatly increased the likelihood that a search would net an illegal firearm. During 1994, officers from the Mobile Reserve Unit made between 5 and 30 consent searches a night. Guns were found in about half of the searches, and nearly three guns per household were seized. All told, the tiny Consent to Search program was responsible for seizing 402 guns in 1994, about half of the total number of guns taken from juveniles by the entire St. Louis Police Department. Even more remarkable for a city with a history of bad blood between the police and members of the black community, 98 percent of those who were asked agreed to allow the police to enter their homes.

Here then was a program that met almost every possible definition of innovation. It began at the grassroots level with a suggestion from a community resident. It was designed carefully and respectfully. Unlike the gun buyback program, it was targeted at the people who were at most risk of killing and being killed. Best of all, it operated at no extra cost to the city.

Fairly quickly, the program started to attract local and national attention. It was nominated by a national policing group for a prestigious innovation award. Risk and another officer traveled to Washington, D.C., to testify about the program before Congress. The program even caught the attention of President Clinton, who viewed it as an example of local innovation (Rosenfeld 2008).

The logical next step was to conduct a formal evaluation of the program. In October 1995, Rosenfeld and Decker were hired by the U.S. Department of Justice to evaluate the program. If it was shown to be effective, there was a strong likelihood that Consent to Search would be adopted by police departments across the country grappling with similar issues of teen violence.

There was just one small problem. When Rosenfeld and Decker began their work a few months later, they discovered that the Consent to Search program had effectively been disbanded.

What happened? The short answer is politics with a small "p." The St. Louis police chief had resigned and was planning to run against the mayor in the next election. The new chief had little incentive to keep programs like Consent to Search up and running because anything associated with the previous police chief (however loose the association) was essentially radioactive. In fact, as part of a reorganization common in police departments, the new chief transferred Risk and other officers involved in the Consent to Search program to different parts of the police department. A new lieutenant was appointed to run the Mobile Reserve Unit. When Rosenfeld and Decker visited him to find out what had happened to the program, the lieutenant at first did not understand what they meant. When the program was described to him, the lieutenant replied that a number of the unit's firearms suppression programs (of which Consent to Search was one example) had been suspended because of "lack of success."

The Consent to Search Program might have been on the verge of becoming a national phenomenon, but very few people in the St. Louis police department knew anything about it. Somehow, news about the program had made its way to President Clinton, but it hadn't traveled from one part of the St. Louis Police Department to another. Mobile Reserve was an isolated unit within the St. Louis Police Department and, on top of that, few officers within the unit participated in the program. Records were kept informally: Sergeant Risk stored completed consent to search forms in a cardboard box that he kept in his basement, which was later destroyed in a flood. Aside from the consent form, Risk and his colleagues had not created any training materials or guidelines that outlined how the program operated. Instead, they relied on their instincts to guide them. This may have been the right decision for getting things done on the street, but it meant that when they left the Mobile Reserve Unit, there was nothing to document that the program had actually existed. And just like that, a seemingly successful innovation disappeared.

## A Second Chance

For most criminal justice innovations, this would have been the end of the road. However, Consent to Search had one unique champion—an official at the National Institute of Justice, Lois Mock, who refused to give up without a fight.

Mock had worked at the National Institute of Justice for many years and was passionate about preventing gun violence. When Rosenfeld and Decker informed her that the Consent to Search program no longer existed, she told them that she would travel to St. Louis to try to get it started up again. "Let's see what we can do," she told Rosenfeld. Together, they tracked down the new police chief at a community meeting. Rosenfeld recalls the unlikely scene of the five-foot-tall Mock striding up to the six-foot, seven-inch police chief and insisting that the program be resurrected. "She told him that the initial program was promising enough to receive funding from the Department of Justice and deserved a second chance," said Rosenfeld (2008). The Chief agreed to revive it, but, as Rosenfeld and Decker write, "only for the purposes of the evaluation, and to avoid embarrassment for the department."

Responsibility for implementing the revived program was given to the newly appointed lieutenant of the Mobile Reserve Unit. Unfortunately, he was clearly uninterested in the program from the beginning. "He called it 'social work,' and not in a good way," said Rosenfeld (2008). In fact, in the months since meeting Rosenfeld and Decker, he had forgotten about the program entirely; the researchers had to show him the *St. Louis Post-Dispatch* article to convince him that it had once operated out of the Mobile Reserve Unit.

The program eventually was rolled out in a very different fashion than it was originally conceived. "It bore almost no resemblance to the original," said Rosenfeld (2008). It no longer would focus on seizing guns; instead, it would seek to arrest offenders. The pledge not to make an arrest, arguably the key component of the initial model, was deleted from the consent form. The lieutenant summed up the philosophy of the reconstituted program by saying, "Why only get a gun with a consent search, when you can get a gun and a criminal with an arrest or search warrant?"

Not surprisingly, consent referrals from the community dried up, and the Unit turned to more traditional enforcement strategies. During 1997, the Unit conducted only 27 consent searches and recovered 31 guns. None of the searches involved young people under the age of 18. "The program had fully subverted its primary goal of reducing the risk of juvenile firearm violence through consent searches," Decker and Rosenfeld (2004) wrote in their follow-up evaluation. After nine months, the program was discontinued.

## A Third Strike

Remarkably, the Consent to Search program had not run out of lives just yet. It would reemerge one final time in late 1998 at the insistence of the U.S. Attorney of the Eastern District of Missouri, Ed Dowd.

Inspired by Operation Ceasefire, a project which successfully halted an epidemic of youth violence in Boston (and which we cover in detail in chapter 3), U.S. Attorneys around the country were seeking to play a more active role in local law enforcement. Dowd, a regular traveler on the conference circuit, had heard a presentation by David Kennedy, a scholar at Harvard University who had helped formulate the Ceasefire strategy. Kennedy was in the habit of citing the St. Louis Consent to Search program as an example of a promising approach to youth violence. Dowd was upset to learn that the program was no longer operating. Recalls Decker, "[Dowd] would say, 'they're talking about this great thing we're doing in St. Louis, and we're not doing it [anymore], and I want to know why!' " (Decker 2008).

By this time, a third police chief had been appointed in St. Louis, and, at Dowd's urging, he agreed to revive the program. Dowd secured funding for the program from the U.S. Department of Justice, and to make sure it was closely supervised, the chief gave it to his Intelligence Unit, located in police headquarters. Sergeant Risk and another officer involved since the program's inception, Sergeant Bob Heimberger, were reassigned to lead the project.

It looked like all the stars were in alignment for the Consent to Search program. The strong support of the U.S. Attorney, along with grant funding, gave it a kind of credibility and legitimacy that it had not enjoyed in the past. And it was being run by two talented officers who had been involved in the project's successful first stage.

Risk and Heimberger quickly set out to correct what they saw as the project's flaws. Officers who agreed to participate received extensive training. Records were kept religiously. Risk and Heimberger knew that some young people were "borrowing" guns kept legally by adults in the house, so they decided to bring along gunlocks and offer training to parents who wanted to make sure their legal firearms were secure. Risk and Heimberger also restored the promise not to prosecute if an illegal firearm was found.

Finally, the officers sought to add a social service component to the project as a means of helping both young people and their often-terrified parents. For Decker, the most wrenching part of Consent to Search was seeing the desperation of the parents they encountered. "I did not expect the level of gratitude the mothers had for what the police were doing," said Decker, who rode along on a number of consent searches. "These mothers had lost control of their kids and needed help" (Decker 2008). Seizing illegal guns from juveniles was still the primary goal of the project, but the officers were not naïve enough to assume that this alone would be enough to alter the trajectories of the families they encountered. Their hope was that more lasting change could be accomplished by linking troubled young people and their parents to social services.

Risk and Heimberger selected a local clergy group, African-American Churches in Dialogue, as a partner. The idea was that officers performing consent searches could refer young people and parents to the group for guidance, support, and links to job training and drug treatment programs.

The intention may have been a good one, but, according to Rosenfeld and Decker, it was a rocky relationship from the beginning. At an initial meeting, one minister asked how they could be sure that the officers would not steal from the homes they were searching. Always quick on his feet, Risk shot back, questioning how the police could be sure that the ministers were not going to molest the young men who were referred to them. The uncomfortable laughter in the room couldn't disguise the implicit lack of trust on both sides.

The program ran four nights a week, from 6 P.M. to 10 P.M. This time, most of the addresses were generated by the Intelligence Unit itself, rather than by referrals from community residents. Risk and Heimberger believed that relying on internal police tips would make the program more effective and reduce the chances of wasted trips. Every morning, they would pore over computerized crime reports, looking for houses to search. At first, clergy members were invited to ride along with the officers, but that practice was quickly abandoned. Heimberger said that officers were uncomfortable in the clergy's presence. "They acted like they didn't trust us," he said (Heimberger 2008). Instead, a referral form was developed that explained the available social services. The police kept a copy for themselves and mailed another copy to the clergy group, with the expectation that its members would follow up with the family.

Before long, however, the police realized that the clergy group was not meeting its end of the bargain. This lack of follow-up was demoralizing to officers like Heimberger, who, to this day, can remember people he encountered on consent searches. "I had one woman tell me, in tears, that she was sure her son was going to be killed," he said. "I don't like that we didn't help her" (Heimberger 2008).

The program in its third iteration suffered from other implementation problems as well. By relying on information generated internally, the police hoped they would be able to better target their resources, yet that decision had the effect of reducing the number of searches performed as well as the chances that parents would consent to a search. From December 1998 to August 1999, a total of 201 consent searches were performed, about half the number conducted in 1994. Strikingly, adults consented to the search in only 42 percent of cases, compared to 98 percent in the project's first stage. "It is not surprising that when parents request the police to come to their residence, they are more likely to grant the police entry," noted Rosenfeld and Decker (2001, 25) dryly. A total of 29 firearms were recovered during this period, a fraction of the 402 guns netted in the program's first phase.

The police believed that one of the most important purposes of the Consent to Search program was symbolic: it offered a visible sign that the St. Louis Police Department cared about communities hit hard by juvenile firearm violence. But the power of symbols only goes so far. The less-than-inspiring statistics, when combined with the lack of follow-up from the clergy group, ultimately crippled the project. The program was terminated when the grant funding expired, and this time for good.

## The Kings of Swamp Castle

In the classic film *Monty Python and the Holy Grail*, the King of Swamp Castle defends his seemingly foolish decision to build his kingdom on shaky ground. "Other kings said I was daft," he tells his son, "but I built it all the same, just to show 'em. It sank into the swamp. So, I built a second one. That sank into the swamp. So, I built a third one. That burned down, fell over, then sank into the swamp" (Monty Python 1975). The officers involved in the St. Louis Consent to Search program could be forgiven if they felt a little like Kings of Swamp Castle.

The truth is that almost every criminal justice innovation is built on a swamp. St. Louis was experiencing an epidemic of youth violence fueled by guns. The police were hard pressed to come up with solutions, particularly in a country where there are almost as many guns in circulation as there are people (Hepburn 2007). It was easy enough to get guns out of the hands of law-abiding individuals via gun buyback programs, but that didn't make a dent in the problem. What's more, the communities with the worst gun violence were those least likely to trust the police. And we haven't even mentioned the lack of job or educational opportunities for young people or the cultural issues (such as the "stop snitching" movement) that complicate efforts to reduce crime in places like St. Louis.

It takes real courage to launch a new program in the face of these kinds of challenges, but that's exactly what a small group of police officers attempted to do in St. Louis. These challenges could derail any initiative, no matter how well conceived or executed. But the St. Louis experiment faced a number of additional obstacles, many of which were self-inflicted. Given the law of unintended consequences, even good (or at least defensible) programmatic choices ended up creating additional problems for the St. Louis reformers.

In its first phase, having the project operate in an isolated unit and keeping procedures relatively informal allowed it to grow and change without interference from police headquarters. It was that very isolation, however, that ended up killing the project—once the officers in charge were transferred, the program effectively ceased to exist. The officers in the third phase decided that relying on internal tips, as opposed to referrals from parents and community members, would allow them to more effectively target their resources. What they did not foresee, however, was how important community referrals were to the legitimacy of the program. As a result, the consent rate for searches dropped from 98 percent to 42 percent. The officers were thoughtful enough to realize that they needed a community partner if they wanted to help terrified parents keep their families safe. But relying on the wrong partner sapped the project's spirit and helped deal it a final blow.

As the tortured history of the Consent to Search program shows, there is no perfect, risk-free way to run a project. It is impossible to say if different decisions could have saved the program. But eliminating failure is an unrealistic goal: the only way to eliminate failure is not to try anything at all. The good news is that success is possible if you embrace failure and learn to see it as a stepping stone rather than as a brick wall; after all, even the King of Swamp Castle was successful on his fourth attempt.

What makes the St. Louis Consent to Search program particularly useful is that it managed to highlight, over the course of its brief and eventful existence, the most common causes of failure in criminal justice reform. In general, there are four types of failure:

- failure of concept (a bad idea)
- failure of implementation (poor execution)
- failure of marketing and politics (an inability to attract the necessary money or manpower)
- failure of self-reflection (reformers becoming so intent in drumming up support for their programs that they fail to assess their own weaknesses or respond as facts on the ground change)

The first, most promising phase of the Consent to Search program is an example of how politics can lead to failure. Given the messy politics of St. Louis, the program's association with the departing chief (and rival to the mayor) was enough to put the initiative on the fast track to oblivion despite its encouraging early track record. Moreover, the isolation of the officers on the Mobile Reserve Unit meant that they had few internal allies that they could rely upon at headquarters to save the program.

Lest we fall into the knee-jerk position that all politics is bad, it is worth highlighting that political forces also brought the Consent to Search program back from the dead. It was, after all, the intervention of an official at the U.S. Department of Justice and later the U.S. Attorney that helped resuscitate the program. Navigating local politics is one of the hardest and most important skills that reformers need to master, a theme we will return to repeatedly throughout this book.

A failure to manage local politics is only part of the Consent to Search story, however. Sometimes, as in the second phase of the Consent to Search program, reforms are killed by bad ideas. Clearly, abandoning the pledge to forgo arrests if illegal contraband was found was not a good idea. It is difficult to imagine even the most talented and dedicated officers making the project work within those constraints. Thus, the second phase of the Consent to Search program ended in failure, just as the first one had, albeit for very different reasons; this time it was a failure not of politics but of concept.

In its third and final stage, the Consent to Search program had the active support of the U.S. Attorney and a dedicated source of grant funding. The political winds seemed to be blowing in the program's direction. The officers involved also had a wealth of good ideas and relevant experiences to draw upon in designing the project. Yet the Consent to Search program failed again, this time because of implementation problems—most notably, the decision to rely on a flawed clergy group as a partner.

In addition to politics, concept, and implementation, there is another source of failure in criminal justice innovation that perhaps is the most important and the least discussed: the failure to engage in reflection and to build knowledge about what works and what doesn't. Here again, the story of the Consent to Search program provides a good example, demonstrating how difficult it is for those in the field of criminal justice to learn from mistakes.

## Failure Redux

The Consent to Search program illustrates the failure of self-reflection in criminal justice because it is such a rarity—a program that yielded a well-written, qualitative analysis of failure. The fact that the report exists in the first place is the product of unique circumstances. Hired to write an evaluation of the Consent to Search program, Rosenfeld and Decker found that the program had been disbanded. Rosenfeld said, "We had no choice but to write about failure" (Rosenfeld 2008).

Rosenfeld and Decker's research is not the final word on the Consent to Search strategy, however. Starting in late 2007, Boston, Washington, D.C., and Philadelphia set out to create their own versions of the program.

Despite having the benefit of the St. Louis experience, each project has struggled to get off the ground, dealing with challenges on multiple fronts, including civil libertarians, community activists, and the National Rifle Association.[2] The key failure in the Washington version of Consent to Search involved marketing: planners failed to generate strong support for the project from local residents and clergy groups before it was announced by the mayor and chief of police. The lack of grassroots political support created an opening for groups like the ACLU, which criticized the program as overly coercive. After weeks of negative press coverage, the department was forced to announce clarifying remarks about the program, which essentially never got off the ground.[3]

Despite the expenditure of thousands of dollars and employee hours in multiple locations, Consent to Search remains what it was when it was first proposed 15 years ago: a promising but unproven strategy to get guns out of the hands of at-risk young people. For their part, Rosenfeld and

Decker freely admit the limitations of their research. They do not know if the Consent to Search program "worked" to reduce violence in St. Louis, a sentiment that Bob Heimberger shares. "I wanted to know the impact of the program beyond the number of guns collected," Heimberger said. "It's a shame, because we could have learned a lot" (Heimberger 2008).

The harsh truth is that, despite important advances in knowledge and practice during the past 20 years, criminal justice agencies are still struggling to understand how to tackle problems like gun violence. According to Michael Scott, a professor at the University of Wisconsin and a former police chief, "In police agencies, we have not developed rigorous standards for defining and measuring success or failure. In their absence, we resort to very personalized and ad-hoc measures. . . . Unfortunately, it's fairly easy to abandon a good idea in policing" (Scott 2008).

To some observers, the contrast between criminal justice and other fields like medicine, where innovations are tested thoroughly before being marketed to the public, is particularly stark. "If an intervention reduced breast cancer by 30 percent, it would quickly become mandated practice, and, conversely, if there was a practice that hurt people, it would be discontinued," said Jeremy Travis, the president of the John Jay College of Criminal Justice and a former Department of Justice official in the Clinton administration. "I can't say the same thing about criminal justice" (Travis 2008).

To be sure, measuring the effects of a complicated, evolving criminal justice experiment like Consent to Search is much more complicated than measuring results in medical research; the latter is more amenable to the gold standard of evaluation research, in which individuals are randomly assigned to experimental and control groups and then carefully tracked. In recent years, an intense debate has erupted among researchers and practitioners about the role research should play in informing criminal justice practice. Some argue that only projects that have already proven their effectiveness (i.e., evidence-based programs) should be supported, while others worry that, if taken too far, the "what works" movement can crowd out innovation and the adoption of new ideas (Smyth and Schorr 2009).

The Consent to Search approach illustrates the complexity of this debate. On one hand, if the government only funded evidence-based programs, Consent to Search never would have been tried in the first place. On the other hand, if the field placed a greater emphasis on evidence, perhaps we would know better whether, why, and under which conditions the Consent to Search strategy works.

## The View from St. Louis

Almost ten years after the Consent to Search program folded for the last time, St. Louis is still a dangerous city, particularly for those who are young and black.[4] Crime rates, which peaked in the early 1990s and then declined for a decade (mirroring national trends), have increased in recent years. There were 138 murders in St. Louis in 2007, up from an average of 113 in the first few years of the new century. As was the case in the early 1990s, violent crime is concentrated in the inner city: half of all homicides occurred in just 12 of St. Louis's 79 neighborhoods. In June 2008, thousands of largely African-American residents marched in protest of the toll that violence was taking on their neighborhoods. They believed the police were doing little to help them.

Like any good innovator, Bob Heimberger, now retired, is still thinking about how the Consent to Search program might have evolved if it had not been shut down. "If there was another gun in the house, would the parent have called us?" he wonders. "Were parents using the safety devices we were offering them? Were we getting guns out of the hands of the right people?" His sharpest regret, however, is losing the chance to see the project evolve and grow. "I thought we were flushing guns out of the houses and into abandoned properties," he said. "It would have been interesting to find out if that was true and figure out how to respond" (Heimberger 2008).

Heimberger is one of the heroes of this book because of his willingness to try something new and engage in a process of trial and error. The real villain in criminal justice is not the threat of failure but acceptance of the status quo.

Like any experienced practitioner, Heimberger can tell his share of stories about the pervasive complacency within the criminal justice system. Before he retired from the police department, Heimberger organized a one-day conference at a local trauma center that was designed to bring together all of the criminal justice and medical personnel who get involved when a young person in St. Louis is shot. His idea was to "reinvestigate" each case from different perspectives to see what lessons could be learned by sharing information across agencies.

The emergency room physicians, schooled in the scientific method, eagerly shared their thoughts and ideas with the group. Halfway through the meeting, however, Heimberger noticed that the commander of the homicide unit was sitting quietly in the back of the room and had not even bothered to take off his hat—a sure sign that he thought the conference was a waste of his time. When Heimberger called on him, the homicide commander held up a tattered copy of a so-called "murder book" that was used to track basic demographic information about murder victims and the officers assigned to investigate such cases. Pointing at it, he told the group dismissively that "if the name's not in the book, then I don't care about it." Those were the only words he spoke in the meeting.

It is safe to say that, unlike Heimberger, the homicide commander did not launch a well-publicized failure in an effort to prevent gun violence. But avoiding failure should not be the goal of the criminal justice system.

# 2

# Failure amid Success

At first glance, judges Bill Meyer and Kevin Burke are unlikely radicals. Very few people make it through law school and onto the bench (Meyer in Denver, Burke in Minneapolis) without a strong faith in American institutions and an ability to work effectively within the status quo. But the goal that Meyer and Burke set for themselves in the mid-1990s was fairly audacious—to overhaul the court system's response to crimes involving drug use.

From their perspective as urban judges, courts across the United States were under siege. In 1980, the police in the United States made a total of 580,900 drug arrests. By 1996, the courts were handling over *1.5 million* drug arrests nationwide, almost a threefold increase.[1]

It wasn't just the flood of drug cases inside the courthouse that troubled Meyer and Burke. Drugs were tearing their communities apart. Crack cocaine had transformed placid Minneapolis into "Murderapolis," in the words of the *New York Times,* after a record 95 people were murdered in 1995, many of them in drug-related shootouts.[2] The situation was no different in Denver, where drug arrests tripled from 1979 to 1993 and a thriving drug trade had made parts of downtown all but uninhabitable.

In 1996, Burke, then the chief judge of the Hennepin County courts in Minnesota, commissioned a study examining how the court system had handled 4,500 annual drug arrests. He was shocked to find that only about 100 defendants were sentenced to state prison. More shocking still was that very few defendants had entered drug treatment. Another problem was delay: most drug cases languished in the system for months or even years without resolution. That meant there were "thousands of people where there was an arrest but nothing ultimately happened," said Burke (2008). "To my mind, this was a lousy criminal justice system."

Back in Denver, Meyer was reaching similar conclusions of his own. "We weren't being very effective in treating the individual who needed treatment," Meyer said. "The serious offender who had possession of large quantities of drugs [would] be on a trial docket with cases involving murder and sexual assault. The crowded nature of the criminal-court docket didn't allow for appropriate attention to the more serious drug cases."[3]

While working in isolation from one another, Burke and Meyer had independently come to the same conclusion: the justice system was not working the way it was supposed to work. They started speaking a truth that many criminal justice officials would acknowledge only behind closed doors. "What was happening with drug cases prior to Kevin [Burke] was atrocious," recalls Toddrick Barnette, who worked in the Minneapolis public defender's office at the time. "I would get a drug case, and for four or five months nothing would happen. Meanwhile, the person would be out in the community, and by the time we got to trial, it was so far down the road we didn't know what to do" (Barnette 2008).

In grasping for a solution to this problem, Burke and Meyer seized on an idea that had been developed a few years earlier in Miami. Known as "drug court," the initiative sought to reduce crime by offering drug offenders judicially mandated drug treatment instead of incarceration. The Miami model had achieved widespread acclaim and helped catapult a local prosecutor named Janet Reno to national prominence. Research suggested that the project reduced both substance abuse and recidivism. Meyer and Burke were keen to bring the drug court concept to Denver and Minneapolis.

For several years, their projects blossomed. The Minneapolis drug court received several awards, including one from the FBI, while Denver's drug court had the support of the editorial pages of the local newspapers and the city's political establishment.

Meanwhile, as attorney general, Janet Reno was using her bully pulpit (and power to dispense federal funding) to promote the expansion of drug courts across the country. Reno's interest in drug courts helped spark a long-lasting commitment by the U.S. Department of Justice. In the years since the Clinton administration, drug courts have proven to be popular with a broad range of political officials, both Democratic and Republican. The U.S. Congress earmarks millions of dollars for drug courts each year. More important, drug courts have proven effective on the ground: they have helped to rehabilitate thousands of addicts and reduced both the use of incarceration and the costs associated with jail and prison (Belenko 2001).

Drug courts are viewed by many scholars as one of the most successful criminal justice innovations of the past 25 years—but not in Denver and Minneapolis. By 2002, Denver's drug court was effectively dead,[4] and the Minneapolis drug court succumbed to a similar fate a few years later.[5]

What went wrong in Denver and Minneapolis? Each city has its own history full of complicated twists and turns. This chapter tells the stories of the drug courts in both cities in an effort to illustrate an important lesson: sometimes good ideas are not enough to guarantee success.

## A New Approach

We could try to help them. This simple idea—that the justice system might aid addicted offenders rather than focus exclusively on punishing them— was what set Judge Herbert Klein of Miami's Eleventh Judicial District on the path toward creating the first drug court (Goldkamp 2003).

The same problems that would overwhelm the Denver and Minneapolis courts in the mid-1990s hit Miami a half decade earlier, during the height of the city's crack-cocaine epidemic. Arrests for drug possession jumped 93 percent from 1984 to 1989, and, according to one study, nearly three-quarters of *all* felony defendants in Miami tested positive for cocaine (Goldkamp 1994). The Miami justice system was caught unprepared. Jail capacity was quickly taxed to the limit. One result was gridlock, as drug cases piled up unresolved: the number of pending felony drug cases increased by 350 percent from 1979 to 1990.[6]

On the surface, Klein's solution to this problem was simple: sentence drug-addicted defendants to treatment instead of jail, and have judges closely monitor their progress. In practice, it was a radical shift—and a risky one. For one thing, it meant involving judges in the messy realities of the treatment process, which often has a "two steps forward, one step back" dynamic as addicts struggle with temptation and relapse. Judges typically don't see defendants after they are sentenced, unless they are rearrested and end up in court again. In drug court, judges monitor cases for at least a year, cajoling defendants in regular status hearings to continue in drug treatment. At times, monitoring also meant tolerating failure, as judges and prosecutors learned the oft-repeated mantra that "relapse is part of recovery." Judges could not simply give up on defendants the first time they tested positive for drugs. "A lot of people here start using again, but they get second, third, and fourth chances from the judge," one Miami prosecutor told a reporter from the *New York Times.* "It is expected that there will be relapses."[7]

The biggest risk, however, was the decision to involve the courts in the rehabilitative business in the first place. The idea that the criminal justice system could rehabilitate offenders had received a battering in the 1970s and 1980s from studies that were interpreted to show that "nothing works" to change the behavior of criminals (Martinson 1974). This conclusion, along with high crime rates, helped fuel a political movement toward more punitive responses to offending (e.g., "three strikes and you're out" laws, mandatory minimums, truth-in-sentencing legislation). By attempting to help defendants become drug free, drug courts were flying in the face of conventional wisdom within the criminal justice system—and the general political mood of the country. "It is easy in retrospect to overlook how dramatic a departure from prevailing judicial philosophy Miami's drug court represented in 1989," writes Temple University professor John S. Goldkamp. "In the larger national court community, Judge Klein's endorsement of treatment as a court strategy, his advocacy of what was received as—how awkward—rehabilitation, was met with uncomfortable silence" (Goldkamp 2003, 197).

Miami's drug court saw cases involving a relatively low-risk group of defendants arrested on first-time felony drug possession charges. (Later, a small number of repeat offenders were added.) In order to "graduate" from drug court, defendants had to complete three phases of treatment: a brief period of detoxification, outpatient drug treatment, and an aftercare component of job training and educational assistance. These three phases were expected to last a year, although a relapse could cause an individual to start the process all over again. In addition, Judge Stanley Goldstein, who was assigned to preside over the Miami drug court, used a series of graduated sanctions and rewards to prod defendants, including two-week motivational jail sentences that he imposed in response to positive drug tests. The drug court offered participants a carrot-and-stick approach. The stick was the prospect of a lengthy jail sentence if the defendant ultimately failed in treatment. Success in treatment, however, would bring a valuable reward: the original charges would be dropped or reduced. This mix of punishment and help appealed to both ends of the liberal-conservative ideological spectrum.

The drug court idea quickly caught on. By 1993, 9 other jurisdictions had opened their own drug courts and 120 had visited Miami to see how the drug court operated. The first drug court evaluation, published in 1993, provided ammunition for drug court advocates: not only did the Miami drug court show modest recidivism declines among participants, but those who were rearrested stayed crime free for two to three times longer than comparison groups.[8] Before long, these positive results caught the attention of two judges in Denver and Minneapolis.

## A Tremendous Force

When they became judges in 1984, neither Bill Meyer nor Kevin Burke could have predicted that they would end up trying to change their local court system's approach to drug offending.

Meyer was known as a brilliant jurist who excelled at resolving complicated cases. "Meyer is one of the three best trial judges I've ever worked with," said Denver prosecutor Greg Long. "He was the type of judge who, if you argued a motion with him . . . would already know the case law and all the precedents." According to Long, the drug epidemic that was eating away at Denver sent Meyer in a very different direction: "Most judges like to deal with more ethereal things involving the law, but this was a cause for Bill. I think drug court fundamentally changed Bill Meyer as a person" (Long 2008).

Before he was appointed to the Minneapolis bench, Kevin Burke had not been particularly interested in becoming a judge. "It was not my life's ambition," he said (Burke 2008). At most, he thought he would spend a few years on the bench before returning to a thriving career in private practice. However, Burke quickly settled into the job and was elected to three terms as assistant chief judge and four terms as chief judge.

Meyer and Burke share many characteristics, including self-confidence in their own analysis and a capacity for relentlessness on behalf of their own ideas. To those who know them, it came as little surprise that they were able to rally support for their drug courts. "Kevin is a tremendous force," said Hennepin County Judge Lucy Wieland, who joined the bench in 1990. "[Drug court] would have never happened without him" (Wieland

2008). In fact, Burke was able to create a system in Hennepin that included three full-time drug court judges, seven dedicated prosecutors, seven defense attorneys, probation officers, and clinical staff.

In Denver, Meyer approached the chief judge of the District Court and convinced him to sign off on drug court. Using a mix of idealism and pragmatism, Meyer argued that drug court was not just the right thing to do, but it would relieve caseload pressure on the other six district court judges by removing drug cases from their dockets. His logic was simple. "To make things work in drug court, I knew I had to show people what was in it for them," Meyer (2008) said. With the help of District Attorney Bill Ritter (now the governor of Colorado), a key early supporter, Meyer obtained federal funds to create a drug court and volunteered to be its first judge.

Although the Miami drug court served as their inspiration, Meyer and Burke both sought to take the Miami model several steps further. Unlike the Miami drug court and almost all other drug courts across the country, the drug courts in Denver and Minneapolis were not restricted to a narrow band of nonviolent, low-level offenders. In addition to handling more cases, both courts were equipped to hold trials, motion hearings, and other proceedings that typically were not part of the drug court model. This translated into enormous caseloads. In contrast to the average drug court, which serves about 93 clients (Bhati, Roman, and Chalfin 2008), the drug courts in Denver and Hennepin County had annual caseloads of between 2,500 and 4,000. "We handled more cases in a week than [some drug courts] handled in a year," said Denver prosecutor Greg Long, who worked in the drug court (Long 2008).

Turning a new idea into reality almost always requires tremendous energy and enthusiasm. In Denver, Judge Meyer was known for starting drug court at 7:00 A.M. and keeping court in session until 7:30 P.M. "I've never worked harder in my life than when I worked in drug court," says Charlie Garcia (2008), a Denver public defender. The payoff for all that hard work could be exhilarating. In Denver, the court held regular "graduation ceremonies" for clients who had completed drug treatment. "When we were rocking and rolling, it was magic," recalls Adam Brickner, a former coordinator of the Denver drug court. "We would graduate 60 to 80 people every six weeks, and those graduations were unbelievably powerful" (Brickner 2008).

Based on research that showed that drug offenders were more likely to complete drug treatment if they were enrolled quickly after an arrest,

Burke set a goal of improving immediacy in Minneapolis. This was a huge change for a jurisdiction in which drug cases could take up to six months to be resolved. Early intervention became the new norm. "A person could be arrested on a Sunday, in drug court on a Monday, and placed in drug treatment by Monday night," recalls drug court coordinator Dennis Miller (2008). This goal, also shared by Bill Meyer, translated into greater efficiency and cost savings in both Minneapolis and Denver. In Minneapolis, the total number of court appearances needed to resolve a drug felony was cut in half, while the lag time between arrest and sentencing dropped sharply, from an average of four to six months to four weeks (Erickson, Welter, and Johnson 1999). In Denver, speedy case processing saved between 7 and 14 days of preconfinement, resulting in annual savings of between $1.8 and $2.5 million in avoided incarceration costs (Granfield, Eby, and Brewster 2002).

## Moving On

In Denver, Judge Bill Meyer stepped down at the end of 1996, after two and a half years as the drug court judge. "Bill recognized that, for drug court to survive, it needed to be more than just his court," said Adam Brickner (2008). There was just one problem: there was no one else in the judiciary who felt as passionately about drug court as Meyer did. "Other judges filled in," said Greg Long (2008), "but none were willing to work as hard as he did."

In truth, even the most committed judge might have found it difficult to step into Meyer's shoes. It quickly became clear that the city did not have the drug treatment capacity to meet the demands of drug court. According to a 2001 study, Colorado ranked next to last among states in terms of the amount of money devoted to alcohol and drug treatment. Colorado allocated only $548,000 in state funding for treatment in 1998, compared to over $11 million in New Mexico. "Drug court is not able to meet its mission," one critic, Christine Donner of the Colorado Criminal Justice Reform Coalition, told a local reporter. "The treatment dollars aren't there."[9]

At the same time, changes in law enforcement threatened to overwhelm a drug court already notable for the size of its caseload. Coors Field, the home of the Colorado Rockies baseball team, opened in downtown Denver in 1995, the year after Denver's drug court was launched.

The opening of the new stadium sparked local redevelopment, as gritty former industrial warehouses were converted into loft apartments. This led to increased enforcement of drug crime as new residents demanded that the police do something about the neighborhood's flourishing drug trade. All told, drug cases represented more than half of Denver's criminal cases in 1996, up from 28 percent in 1993 (Hoffman 2002). This increased the pressure on the drug court because, in effect, a single judge was handling half of all felony arrests in Denver.

By 1999, the drug court was handling 95 cases per day, which included new arraignments, status hearings, and trials. "Managing that docket became all encompassing," said former coordinator Adam Brickner (2008). "It was hard on judges, who weren't used to that kind of caseload." At first, the judges who followed Meyer were asked to sit in drug court for a short period and then they would return to their regular courtrooms. Within a few years, it became hard to find judges to volunteer for the position. "Except for its Herculean founder, no judge has been able to remain in the Denver Drug Court for more than one year," wrote Denver District Court Judge Morris Hoffman (2002, 1504), a persistent critic.

The drug court responded by trying to reduce caseload pressure. In so doing, however, it undermined the original "take all comers" philosophy. For example, in February 1997, Judge John Coughlin, who was Meyer's successor, announced plans to cut the drug court caseload by 25 percent by excluding illegal immigrants and two-time felons, a decision that disheartened some of the earliest supporters of drug court. "We started to cherry-pick the population," said public defender Charles Garcia (2008). In addition, the court hired two part-time magistrates (quasi-judicial officers who can carry out some but not all of the functions of a judge) to take on some of the responsibilities of drug court judges, such as monitoring individuals in treatment.

An even more fundamental change was announced in May 2000: initial hearings for all drug cases were transferred out of Denver's district court, where the drug court was located, to the county court. The county court's role was to separate those drug cases in which a defendant was willing to plead guilty and enter treatment from those in which a defendant intended to pursue trial. If a trial was likely, the defendant would go to another district court instead of drug court. In many respects, this decision made sense, because it allowed the treatment court to focus its attention on supervising offenders in drug treatment. One of the casualties of this decision, however, was the principle of immediacy and early intervention, as weeks were added to the process of getting defendants into treatment.

Even with these changes, it was clear that the drug court was buckling under the strain of its enormous caseload. For example, bench warrants, which are issued when a defendant fails to appear in court, began to pile up, a result not only of the volume of drug court cases but of the number of ongoing appearances that a drug court required in comparison to a typical criminal court. The drug court was creating additional opportunities for offenders to fail, an example of the law of unintended consequences. According to Morris Hoffman, some of the judges who succeeded Meyer set limits on the number of cases they would hear that involved individuals returned to court on a warrant, which meant that defendants could spend as long as two to three weeks in jail before seeing a judge (Hoffman 2000).

The struggles that the Denver drug court experienced eventually spilled over to the rest of the district court, which was now handling trials, motions, and other matters for which Meyer had previously assumed responsibility. "The Denver Drug Court has increased, rather than decreased, the workloads of the other [courtrooms]," Hoffman argued (Hoffman 2002).

In retrospect, it seems clear that support in Denver's judiciary for the drug court was never terribly deep. "The [lack of buy-in] was a failure right from the beginning," said Denver prosecutor Greg Long (2008). "[The other] judges felt like drug court was Bill Meyer's baby," said Denver drug court coordinator Adam Brickner (2008). "It wasn't something that they supported." While most judges kept their criticisms private, Judge Morris Hoffman became an outspoken critic, penning a scathing law review article titled "The Drug Court Scandal" and later claiming that the "Denver experiment has gone horribly wrong" (Hoffman 2002).

For Meyer and Ritter, this turn against drug court was a deeply frustrating experience. In 2001, the two men published an article that addressed Hoffman's criticisms, pointing to evidence that showed that the drug court was modestly successful in reducing recidivism and encouraging offenders to stay in treatment over the long haul (Meyer and Ritter 2002). "I'm not saying drug court is perfect, but it's better than anything else out there," Meyer told a Denver reporter. "It's certainly better than anything the naysayers on the district court have come up with."[10]

Meyer's efforts came too late, however. When federal funding expired in 2002, the district court took the opportunity to scale back drug court significantly. Instead of a drug court judge hearing all drug cases, these cases would be distributed evenly over Denver's seven courtrooms, with two part-time magistrates available to monitor a limited number of referred defendants on an as-needed basis. It was a bitter disappointment for some of the most passionate and powerful supporters of the drug court. In a lengthy profile published in the *Denver Post* on the eve of his successful run for governor in 2006, Ritter cited a failure to obtain "political buy-in" from the bench for drug court as his greatest regret as Denver's district attorney.[11]

## A Perfect Storm in Minneapolis

In Minneapolis, opposition to drug court came from another quarter: the law enforcement community.

From the beginning, Judge Burke's approach to running a drug court differed from the model's founders in Miami. In Miami, the drug court was intentionally nonadversarial—in other words, instead of being pitted against each other, once a defendant agreed to enter the program, prosecutors and defense attorneys focused on a shared goal of helping participants become drug free. One way the Miami drug court reduced adversarialism was to require that all defendants plead guilty as a condition of receiving drug treatment, which meant that questions of guilt and innocence had essentially been decided before the drug court took the case. As a consequence, considerable discretion was placed in the hands of prosecutors, who could dictate which defendants were eligible for drug treatment and which were not. The drug court worked hard to resolve potential areas of disagreement before they hit the courtroom.

Burke had no intention of adopting a nonadversarial, "team" approach to drug court. Unlike in Miami, all drug offenders in Minneapolis, including the most serious first- and second-degree felons, were eligible to be assessed for drug treatment. Burke believed that judges should not give prosecutors too much power in deciding who was an appropriate candidate for drug court. This meant that Burke and his successors often sentenced defendants to drug treatment over the vociferous complaints of prosecutors, who wanted prison sentences.[12] In addition, Burke allowed defendants to enter drug treatment while still preserving their full trial rights. This was an important point of principle for Burke, who believed that "inner-city black persons should not be asked to choose between treatment and their constitutional rights" (Burke 2008).

Almost inevitably, these deviations from the Miami model led to tensions in the courtroom. Gail Baez, a prosecutor in the Hennepin County drug court, said, "From the standpoint of a prosecutor, we had no ability to control cases" (Baez 2008). Prosecutorial grumbling soon led to the idea that the drug court was "soft" on defendants, a crippling perception problem. As long as Burke was on the bench, these simmering tensions could be managed, but it was a different story when he left the drug court in 2000. "The judges that handled [cases after Burke] really lost credibility with law enforcement and the community," Baez said. "There was constant seething and anger around here" (Baez 2008). As was the case in Denver, the departure of the original judge ended up dealing a heavy blow to drug court, exposing controversial program policies and fault lines that, in truth, had existed from the very start.

After Burke left, police and prosecutors went from being privately opposed to being vocal critics of the drug court, according to drug court coordinator Dennis Miller (2008). In fact, some of the drug court's most important initial selling points—its comprehensive approach to drug offending and its capacity to rapidly process cases—ended up being used against it. "I was distressed and mortified when I started in drug court and saw the way dispositions were being handled," said Baez (2008). The perception was that "anybody and everybody" got into drug court. Baez's colleague, Jane Ranum, who returned to the Hennepin County District Attorney's Office in 2006 after 16 years in the state legislature, shared her view. "I was absolutely shocked," Ranum said. "Judges were giving [drug treatment] sentences to people who were clearly violent" (Ranum 2008).

Police officers also came to resent what they saw as the revolving door of drug court. "Everybody went into the drug court system, [only] to be released a few hours later," said Lieutenant Marie Przynski (2008) of the Minneapolis Police Department. "The drug court didn't distinguish between the drug dealer and the drug user."

These concerns eventually exploded into public view. Przynski recalls inviting a drug court judge to attend a community meeting in April 2002 that was filled with local residents who wanted to express their anger with the drug court. "The judge deserves a medal of courage for attending the meeting," she said (Przynski 2008). Katherine Kersten, a conservative columnist for the *Minneapolis Star-Tribune,* even blamed drug court for contributing to a 15 percent rise in violent crime in Minneapolis in 2005. Kersten quoted a police officer on the city's gang task force who said, "Drug Court is killing us. Drugs are behind a lot of the crime in this city. But today we arrest drug dealers, and they're right back on the street." Among the officer's incendiary charges was that a well-known drug dealer had received only a few weeks in jail from drug court after being arrested on five separate felony offenses.[13]

Over time, the drug court lost the support of key local officials, including the mayor, the county prosecutor, and the chief public defender. "It was a perfect storm," said Burke (2008). "All the players changed, and they weren't supportive." According to Lucy Wieland, who succeeded Burke as chief judge of Hennepin County in 2004, drug court had become a political liability. "Elected officials and the police were really unhappy" (Wieland 2008).

Burke considers the soft-on-crime criticism to be unfair. For example, it turned out that the drug offender cited in the column critical of the drug court had served 400 days in jail, not 40 days, and Burke got the newspaper to print a small retraction (Burke 2008). It is true that, generally speaking, judges in Minnesota (which has one of the lowest incarceration rates in the country) are loath to send drug offenders to state prison (Warren 2008). The unpopular practice of drug court judges "departing" from the sentencing recommendations of prosecutors was not unique to drug court or even to Hennepin County. "Before the drug court, [drug offenders] weren't going to prison," said Wieland (2008). "The departure rate for drug offenses is extremely high across the state."

Still, the truth was that in Hennepin County, perception had become reality. Beneath the surface of the law enforcement critiques was another troubling reality: after almost a decade of operations, the drug court was coming apart at the seams. At its height, the drug court was managing a caseload of about 4,000 participants. Every probation officer had more than 200 cases, an unmanageable number. "Over time, we got bigger, but our budget didn't grow to keep up," said Dennis Miller (2008). Decisions were increasingly made on an ad hoc basis. "There was no filtering out of whether a person was an addict or a drug dealer, whether a person was chemically dependent or chemically abusive," said Toddrick Barnette (2008), who worked as a public defender in the drug court.

In 2005, Judge Wieland invited Ed Latessa, a professor at the University of Cincinnati, to evaluate the drug court as part of a countywide task force on chemical dependency she was cochairing. His assessment was withering. "The drug court tried to be everything to everybody," he said, "but the outcomes were abysmal" (Latessa 2008).

After over a decade of operations, it was also unclear what effect, if any, the drug court had on recidivism: the only study to explore the question had found that drug court participants were slightly *more* likely to be rearrested than a comparison group, although the difference was statistically insignificant (Ericson, Welter, and Johnson 1999).

Over the course of a decade, the Hennepin County drug court had followed an unfortunate trajectory. As Barnette recalls, by the time he joined drug court as a public defender, the initial spark that had powered the program was gone. "I don't think that [the players in court] had the same idea, or a good idea, [as to] why this particular drug court should work for these defendants," he said. "I didn't feel like we had a purpose" (Barnette 2008).

In 2008, Judge Wieland announced plans to radically restructure the drug court, limiting eligibility to a small number of offenders who had been identified as chemically dependent and at risk of future offending.[14] Instead of a drug court system hearing all drug cases, Minneapolis would limit its effort to a single courtroom, with a few hundred cases at most. Judge Burke's ambitious vision of drug court was dead.

## The Politics of Criminal Justice Reform

The idea of an independent, apolitical judiciary is a strong one in this country. To many observers, politics and the courts are the equivalent of oil and water—two elements that should never mix. For example, the Conference of Chief Judges and the American Bar Association (ABA) strongly oppose the practice of judicial elections, which (in the ABA's words) "threaten the public's trust and confidence in our state courts." According to the ABA's analysis, the problem is that involving judges in the political process "blurs the lines between the role of judges as impartial arbiters and the political role of lawmakers and executive branch officials." As a result, "the public begins to view judges as being just like any other politicians" (American Bar Association 2008).

The notion that the courts function best when they are basically apolitical has a long history. For example, Alexander Hamilton famously characterized the judiciary as the "least dangerous branch" of government, lacking the executive branch's power to command armies and the legislative branch's power over budgets. Hamilton's words have been invoked countless times as a reminder that, to survive, the courts must be seen by the public as impartial arbiters who are capable of rising above petty politics.

To Kevin Burke, however, the view that politics and courts do not mix is misguided if taken to an extreme. "Opposition to a political judiciary makes sense if you assume politics is a bad thing," he said. "But if you see politics as the art of creating a vision and motivating people towards your vision, then a political judiciary is a good thing" (Burke 2008).

The Denver and Minneapolis drug courts are good examples of the role that politics—in the sense of organizing, coalition building, and responding to the concerns of the community—plays in criminal justice reform. Meyer and Burke brought more than the ability to write a well-crafted decision to the task of addressing the problem of drug-fueled crime in Denver and Minneapolis; they brought the capacity to pull the levers of power, moving people and processes in a direction that was consistent with their vision. In other words, they brought enormous political skill. Their efforts are all the more impressive given how hard it can be to get courts to change how they operate. Burke observes that "the judiciary is an inherently conservative organization, which makes risk-taking difficult" (Burke 2008).

The justice system is no different than any other field of human endeavor. Good ideas are not enough—you have to be strategic and figure out how to move the system. Politics with a small "p" matters. As we saw in chapter 1 with the checkered history of Consent to Search, politics can save or kill a program. So it would be with the Denver and Minneapolis drug courts. If their initial success was driven in no small measure by the political acumen of their charismatic founders, their ultimate failure also was driven by political concerns. In Denver and Minneapolis, Bill Meyer and Kevin Burke were able to get drug courts started through the sheer force of their will. But they were not able to cobble together the kind of lasting coalitions necessary for the drug courts' long-term survival. When presented with the opportunity to end the drug court, the judges in Denver and the police and prosecutors in Minneapolis did just that. Meyer's and Burke's political coalitions simply weren't strong enough.

The collapse of support for the Denver and Minneapolis drug courts was in large part a failure of planning for succession. The departure of the founders was a debilitating blow in light of the symbolic and practical power of the drug court judge. For example, in Denver, it turned out that support for drug court rested on an exceedingly fragile foundation: the willingness of Bill Meyer to work heroically long hours. "Every year after Bill left, they would rotate in a different judge," said Denver public defender Charles Garcia (2008). "None had the commitment that he did."

Denver prosecutor Helen Morgan agreed that drug court "cannot be centered on one or two personalities. It has to be a program where new people can come in and flourish" (Morgan 2008). That was not the case in Denver. "The lesson [learned from Denver's drug court] is that it can't be on one person's shoulders," said court administrator Miles Flesche. "[The drug court] would have had an easier transition if Meyer had involved more judges" (Flesche 2008).

Time and again, reform initiatives are hobbled by an inability to solve problems of succession. The founders of any successful innovation eventually will move on, whether willingly or unwillingly. But many programs fail to plan for this eventuality. In a review of failed policing initiatives, Professor Wesley Skogan of the University of Chicago lists leadership transitions as a key source of failure. "If reforms are to persist," Skogan concludes, "the astute change manager has to ensure that they are the department's and even the city's project, not just their own" (Skogan 2008, 33).

The Denver and Minneapolis experiments might have survived the departure of their founders and the fragile nature of their political coalitions if the drug courts had stronger designs and operational protocols. According to scholar Ed Latessa, the Minneapolis drug court failed to target its resources to drug-addicted felons who could benefit the most from mandated treatment. "After spending a half day up there, it was very obvious to me that [the drug court] wasn't effective," he said (Latessa 2008). Drug court coordinator Dennis Miller agrees with Latessa's assessment. "I think it's true that we were overserving low-risk people and underserving high-risk people," he said. According to Miller, the decision to treat all participants in the same way meant the drug court did not target its limited resources effectively. "We had people in our drug court program showing up for drug testing and more frequent court appearances that were not likely to offend," he said. "They were involved in a program that was too demanding. We also had people who were very likely to reoffend, yet, with high caseloads, we were unable to do the kind of community supervision that was necessary" (Miller 2008).

According to Burke, prosecutors in Minneapolis objected to the inclusion of first- and second-degree felons in the drug court almost from the beginning. As long as Burke was on the bench, this disagreement could be finessed because of the respect prosecutors had for him. Once he left, however, the situation changed. Likewise, Meyer never would compromise his vision of a court that provided comprehensive coverage of all drug cases, even though it meant the drug court followed a backbreaking and ultimately unsustainable work schedule.

## I Wouldn't Call It a Failure

By 2008, over 2,100 drug courts had opened across the country, serving nearly 70,000 adult and juvenile offenders. Study after study has shown that well-implemented drug courts reduce recidivism, save money, and rescue lives from the downward spiral of addiction and crime. Estimates of recidivism reductions range from 8 to 29 percent.[15] According to a report from the Urban Institute, drug courts return a benefit of $2.21 for every dollar spent, for an annual net benefit to society of $624 million (Bhati et al. 2008). Drug court is, in sum, the rarest of commodities: a criminal justice reform that actually works.

Positive research findings have helped earn drug courts powerful endorsements from the national media, including favorable coverage from the *New York Times*[16] and *USA Today*.[17] Drug courts have received support from both sides of the political aisle, which has translated into generous federal government funding; since the passage of the 1994 crime bill, hundreds of millions of dollars have flowed from Washington to drug courts nationwide. This bipartisan support was highlighted when both John McCain and Barack Obama endorsed drug courts during the 2008 presidential election.

Denver and Minneapolis are two prominent exceptions to the rule of widespread drug court success, throwing into sharp relief the achievements of most drug courts, which have successfully addressed such issues as the departure of charismatic judges, the perception of treatment as soft on crime, and the need to create protocols and procedures to ensure effectiveness over the long haul.

To be fair, the drug courts in Denver and Minneapolis still exist, albeit in very different forms. In 2007, the Denver city council provided $1.2 million to revive the moribund drug court. The idea behind the new model was to empower magistrates to handle drug court cases, giving them the ability to sentence defendants to probation. According to prosecutor Helen Morgan, the drug court was established with the lessons from the earlier failure in mind. For one thing, by making magistrates responsible for drug court, Denver sidestepped the problem of a lack of judicial support for the model. "People apply for the position of drug court magistrate," she said. "That's what they want to do." In addition, according to Morgan, Denver has worked carefully to develop a set of protocols and agreements on how the drug court is to operate. The goal is to insulate the Denver drug court from the changes that can occur when key personnel move on. "You're always going to have one or two driving personalities [who make innovation happen]," said Morgan. "That's fabulous, but you know those people aren't going to be around forever. Today, if a new probation chief comes in and tries to change [the] priorities [of the drug court], we can point to the commitments that have already been made" (Morgan 2008).

A much smaller version of drug court also still operates in Hennepin County, presided over by a former prosecutor, Pete Cahill. With a single dedicated judge and well-crafted eligibility guidelines, it looks more like a typical drug court and appears to have the widespread support of the legal community.

Although the drug courts in Denver and Minneapolis have been revived, they are smaller and more modest than the original models devised by Meyer and Burke. As Hennepin County District Court Judge Gary Larson, who presided over the original version of the Hennepin County drug court, asks, "Is the community better off with a drug court with 4,000 people [in drug treatment] doing B-minus work, or a drug court with 100 people in it doing A-plus work?" (Larson 2008). It is a tough question to answer.

Still, it is worth noting that, for all their problems, the Denver and Minneapolis drug courts enjoyed a relatively long life. For that reason, Burke is reluctant to label his drug court a failure. "I wouldn't call it a failure," he said. "Its run in Hennepin County was longer than most Broadway shows. Do you think *The Producers* was a failure? Maybe what the criminal justice system needs are more successful plays that eventually close, as opposed to mediocre ones that just go on and on" (Burke 2008).

# 3

# The Complicated Legacy
# of Operation Ceasefire

David Kennedy, a professor at John Jay College, has taken an unconventional path to academic stardom. Unlike most academics, he never earned an advanced degree. After graduating with a B.A. in philosophy and history from Swarthmore College in 1980, Kennedy began writing case studies at Harvard University's John F. Kennedy School of Government. Although he had no particular interest in policing, Kennedy was assigned a case study on the Los Angeles Police Department's effort to control crack cocaine markets in the city's public housing projects. "That got me into some of the worst housing projects and crack markets in South Central," Kennedy recalled (2008).

His interest piqued, Kennedy volunteered to work on a project closer to home. During the 1990s, Boston was plagued by a series of homicides involving young people (Kennedy, Braga, and Piehl 2001). The sense among many residents and the police was that some Boston neighborhoods were in the grip of an epidemic of drugs and violence. Things were spiraling out of control.

"We were responding to six, seven shootings every night," said Lieutenant Detective Gary French, the head of the Boston Police Department's Youth Violence Strike Force. "You just ran from crime scene to crime scene." Gangs and gang violence appeared to be unmanageable. One district court judge even called for the deployment of the National Guard to prevent gangs from intimidating witnesses during trials. "I think there

45

was a real question in people's minds about whether Boston would remain a viable city," said Paul Evans, the city's police chief (Kennedy et al. 2001).

Boston's effort to combat gang violence was called Operation Ceasefire. Launched in 1995, Operation Ceasefire turned into one of the most celebrated criminal justice initiatives of the past 25 years. Working alongside experienced police and probation officers, Kennedy and two colleagues at Harvard implemented a targeted law enforcement strategy that led to a 63 percent drop in homicides among young people. Overall, murders in Boston dropped from 152 in 1990 to 31 in 1999.

Newspapers were quick to hail the "Boston miracle." President Clinton used Boston as a backdrop to announce a major new youth violence prevention initiative, and Kennedy was invited to visit the White House five times in a two-year period. The phone rang off the hook, and visitors from around the country and the world came to Boston to learn the city's secrets. "The public atmosphere around Ceasefire was nothing anyone had seen before," said Kennedy. "There's probably nothing like it in the history of criminology" (Kennedy 2008).

It was easy to see why Ceasefire captured the imagination of both the public and criminal justice officials. For one thing, the project was run on nothing more than a small planning grant from the National Institute of Justice. The core insight of Ceasefire was that the youth homicide problem in Boston, far from being unmanageable, could be traced to a very small number of young people in a small number of gangs. This meant that the police did not have to use traditional enforcement strategies (such as massive police sweeps) that often attract community opposition. Instead, they could use more precise strategies aimed at those individuals who were responsible for most of the violence. As a result, instead of protests, Operation Ceasefire had the endorsement of numerous prominent African-American clergymen, including Eugene Rivers, who was profiled by *Newsweek* in a cover article (Leland 1998). In short, Operation Ceasefire offered a solution to Boston's crime problem and a way to heal racial tensions at the same time—and did it on the cheap.

Operation Ceasefire was a turning point in David Kennedy's career. Before long, he started traveling the country to promote the ideas pioneered in Boston, including helping law enforcement officials in Minneapolis, Indianapolis, and other cities implement their own versions of Ceasefire. The federal government threw its weight behind the Boston model, launching a 10-site project designed to replicate Operation Ceasefire.

There was only one problem. The success that had turned Kennedy, Rivers, and their colleagues into criminal justice celebrities was tearing the project apart. At the height of its national reputation, Operation Ceasefire collapsed in Boston, amid vicious squabbling over who deserved credit. The murder rate in Boston started to creep back up. The miracle had become undone.

The collapse in Boston threatened to tarnish the ideas behind the project and the Ceasefire brand. One prominent project in Chicago took the name Operation CeaseFire, even though it had a different focus and different operational protocols than the Boston project. In addition, some high-powered academics, noting that the original Operation Ceasefire had never been subjected to rigorous evaluation, began to cast doubt on the project's effectiveness (Wellford, Pepper, and Petrie 2004).

The challenge for Kennedy and for those who cared about the ideas behind Ceasefire was stark. Would the public controversy over Ceasefire take the underlying strategy down with it? When all is said and done, Ceasefire is a story about the challenges of replication, the difficulties of interagency collaboration, and the disconnect between researchers and practitioners.

## The Boston Story

Operation Ceasefire was the product of a set of fortunate circumstances, a combination of thoughtful strategy and good timing. Most importantly, by the time Kennedy and his two Harvard colleagues, Anthony Braga and Annie Piehl, came upon the scene, there were already a small number of dedicated and knowledgeable law enforcement officials in a special police unit that was working on the problem of gang and youth violence in one of Boston's most dangerous neighborhoods.

The unit's leader was Detective Sergeant Paul Joyce. Joyce had seen the futility of more traditional law enforcement techniques, such as massive stop-and-frisk tactics which generated a firestorm of criticism from the press and leaders of the African-American community. Named to head a special unit called the Youth Violence Strike Force, Joyce deliberately sought to forge a new path. "We'd been out there trying to do this on our own, the only way we knew how, and it just hadn't worked," Joyce said. "It taught us that we couldn't do it alone and we couldn't do it without support from the community and other agencies. And that it couldn't be just policing, or just enforcement; there had to be prevention, too" (Kennedy et al. 2001, 10).

With that lesson in mind, Joyce recruited a remarkably diverse coalition of representatives of other law enforcement agencies as well as less typical partners. These partners included street-based outreach workers (known as "streetworkers") employed by the city to work directly with at-risk young people as well as members of the Ten Point Coalition, a group of activist African-American clergy formed after a particularly horrific gang shootout had erupted at a funeral held at a local church.

Even before the Harvard researchers came along, Joyce's efforts had produced some early results, based more on informal improvisation than any strategic plan. For example, police officers on the Youth Violence Strike Force began riding along with probation officers in an effort to jointly enforce conditions of probation, including curfews and area restrictions. "We never used to leave the office or talk to the police," recalled one probation officer. "But . . . we realized we were all dealing with the same kids. And one day, they said, do you want to ride together?" (Kennedy et al. 2001, 11–12).

This seemingly simple step had immediate results. On the first night of the program, which later became known as Operation Night Light, the police were able to solve a shooting because many of the witnesses were on probation and were out long past their curfew. By cooperating with the police, the witnesses were able to avoid being sent back to prison for violating the terms of their probation (Kennedy et al. 2001).

Despite these early wins, it was clear that the problem of youth homicide hadn't been solved. That's where Kennedy and his colleagues came in. They volunteered to pull together the members of Joyce's ad hoc coalition into a more formal working group and help design a more coherent strategy. Joyce welcomed the Harvard researchers with open arms. Still, it was not clear what, if anything, would change with the arrival of the Harvard researchers. After all, the problems facing inner-city Boston seemed hopeless. "I didn't think there was anything that could be done to stop the violence," said one working group participant. "I just didn't see how you could do it" (Kennedy et al. 2001, 12).

On the surface, what Kennedy and his colleagues contributed was exactly what you might expect from a group of Harvard researchers: a focus on data and analysis. Their first step was to point out that, far from being a widespread problem, youth violence was, in fact, remarkably concentrated: a small number of young people were responsible for the lion's share of the problem. The method they used to arrive at this conclusion was simple. In multiple sessions with members of the working group, they wrote down everything anyone knew about the 155 young people murdered in Boston from 1991 to 1994. In about 70 percent (107) of the murders, it turned out that the members of the collaborative had considerable information about the crimes, far more than what had been recorded in any official reports. When the researchers added up all that was known about these 107 incidents, they came up with some startling findings. Ninety of the 107 known incidents were classified by the group as gang-related. They next identified 61 gangs involved in the violence, and these gangs comprised about 1,300 members. This effectively meant that about 1 percent of young people citywide were responsible for nearly 60 percent of the city's youth homicides (Kennedy, Braga, and Piehl 1997).

Their analysis did not stop there. It turned out that both homicide victims and offenders were well known to the criminal justice system, long before the crimes took place. For example, over three-quarters of the victims and offenders in their sample had been arraigned for at least one offense prior to the homicide. Of this group, the average number of arraignments was 9.5 for victims and 9.7 for offenders. That meant that both the victim and the offender had already been arrested *more than nine times* before the murder took place. Perhaps not surprisingly, more than half of offenders had been on probation, and 26 percent were on probation *at the time* they murdered another young person. For victims, the corresponding numbers were 42 and 14 percent (Kennedy 1997).

All of this suggested that a very small number of young people, already enmeshed in the criminal justice system, were extraordinarily at risk of killing or being killed. According to the analysis of the Harvard team, a gang member in a troubled neighborhood had about a one in seven chance of becoming a murder victim.

The members of the working group, which included a broad range of voices, were surprisingly empathetic towards the plight of these young people given the damage they were causing. The working group understood that most of the gangs were not large criminal enterprises, but smaller groups that offered a sense of community to troubled young people. While some of the murders were motivated by disputes over turf, most came from personal "beefs" between members of different gangs. As one street-based outreach worker put it, "Civil society has broken down on the streets. We are utterly failing to protect these kids and so they've reverted to a state of nature. Unless we can reimpose civil society, we're not going to make a lot of headway" (Kennedy et al. 2001).

Seen one way, the fact that so many young victims and offenders were already known to the criminal justice system was a symbol of failure, of the utter futility of trying to stop a pattern of criminality. To the members of the Operation Ceasefire working group, however, it represented an opportunity. According to Kennedy, the working group saw that "gangs and gang members left themselves open to an enormous number of sanctions, exactly *because* they were so criminal. . . . There was, in short, an enormous sanctioning power that the enforcement community could bring to bear against particular gangs and gang members" (Kennedy 1997).

Considered alone, this was not a particularly new insight. What was different about Ceasefire was the manner in which the criminal justice system's enforcement powers would be used. Guided by the research, the members of the working group would seek to convince at-risk young people that it was in their self-interest to stop killing one another. The Harvard researchers referred to their strategy as "pulling levers."

Although many of the levers that would end up being pulled in Boston were traditional law enforcement techniques, such as enforcing conditions of probation or vigorously prosecuting even minor offenses committed by gang members, the key element of the Ceasefire approach came straight from Madison Avenue. Prodded by Kennedy, the working group came to realize that what they were attempting was basically a targeted marketing strategy. Their product was safety and security, and they were trying to sell it to a niche audience that had little confidence in the quality of the product being offered.

## "We Were Honest with Them"

As part of their work, Kennedy and his Harvard colleagues interviewed Detective Sergeant Joyce and other members of the Youth Violence Strike Force to understand the history of the gang violence problem in Boston. One police operation in particular, aimed at the Wendover Street gang, kept coming up in conversation. At first glance, it seemed like a fairly typical initiative: Joyce's team had worked in collaboration with the federal Bureau of Alcohol, Tobacco, and Firearms to shut down an illegal gun trafficking ring that was supplying guns to the gang. Yet, the more Kennedy learned, the more he realized there was another, equally important strategy that the unit had pursued.

The key clue came from a cryptic comment made by Joyce: "We were honest with them." What Joyce meant was that, in addition to developing a case against the gun traffickers, the Youth Violence Strike Force had aggressively pursued any legal strategy they could think of against gang members and took pains to explain to the gang what they were doing and why. This included everything from digging up outstanding warrants and having them enforced to seizing the cars of unlicensed drivers. In one instance, the unit discovered that a gang leader was under the supervision of the Department of Youth Services; with their cooperation, they had the young person shipped off to a facility in Western Massachusetts. To paraphrase Kennedy, the message of the police was, "We're here because of the violence, and we'll make your life hell until it stops." Even more important than the specifics of the message was the fact that it was delivered in direct conversations between the police and gang members. As commonsensical as it may seem, the idea was decidedly unconventional. Instead of assuming that a law enforcement action would "speak for itself," the police were taking the time to make sure that their message was getting across to gang members.

The strategy appeared to pay off: in addition to successful prosecutions against traffickers, a number of Wendover Street gang members had taken the extraordinary step of *voluntarily* turning in their guns to the police.

Of course, the question was whether an approach taken against a single gang in a single neighborhood would work if it were carried out more broadly. During late 1995 and early 1996, the Harvard researchers began making presentations to members of the working group to explain the strategy. Joyce reached out to key partners, including the clergy and judicial leaders, to describe the new approach. The response, which was overwhelmingly positive, reflected how desperate the situation seemed to these leaders at the time: things were so bad that it could not be made any worse.

The working group eventually concentrated their attention on two gangs: the Intervale Posse and the Vamp Hill Kings. Working with the U.S. Drug Enforcement Agency, Joyce had been building a case against the Intervale Posse, considered one of the most dangerous gangs in Boston. As the case was being put together, violence broke out among members of the other gang, the Vamp Hill Kings, which operated out of the Dorchester neighborhood. Three gang members were murdered as a result of intragang squabbles. This crime provided the first practical test of the "pulling levers" strategy. Using many of the strategies developed earlier with the Wendover Street gang, the working group used every tool at their disposal to put pressure on the Vamp Hill Kings, at one point even using the Massachusetts Society for the Prevention of Cruelty to Animals to remove pit bulls trained as fighting dogs.

The real innovation, however, came in how the working group communicated what they were doing to the people they were trying to affect. In mid-1996, they invited a dozen leading members of the Vamp Hill Kings to a courthouse in Dorchester. When the gang members arrived, they were greeted by the members of the working group, who explained in a clear, direct way the range of law enforcement penalties that could be used against gang members. To help make the threat tangible, they passed out a piece of paper summarizing the experience of a gang member who had been sentenced to prison for 19 years after being caught with a single bullet. The forum also included an offer of help: a street-based outreach worker who was familiar to many of the gang members made an impassioned plea for the violence to stop and promised to help gang members in any way he could.

The carrot-and-stick message was driven home still further in August 1996, when the long-planned operation against the Intervale Posse finally paid off. Over 20 members of the gang were charged with drug trafficking crimes. The arrests generated extensive media coverage. In meetings with arrested gang members, one-on-one conversations on the streets, and community forums, the working group emphasized that the operation was aimed at the violent behavior of the gang. The headline of a flyer produced by the working group read, "They Were Warned; They Didn't Listen."

A crucial element of the strategy was message discipline. Ceasefire required extraordinary cooperation among members of the working group. For example, in late May, U.S. Attorney Donald Stern convened a meeting with about 40 street-based outreach workers. As Kennedy recalls, many of the outreach workers, skeptical about law enforcement approaches in general, challenged Stern about whether he would be cracking down harshly on minor drug users. Stern's reply was direct. "No," he said. "This is about *violence*. Only the key players in the most violent groups have to worry" (Kennedy et al. 2001, 40). The outreach workers walked away satisfied and agreed to spread the word through their local networks.

The arrests of Intervale Posse gang members appeared to be a turning point. For Gary French, who had replaced Paul Joyce as head of the Youth Violence Task Force (Joyce was promoted within the department in early 1996), the most tangible evidence that something had changed was that his beeper, which used to buzz constantly to alert him to another criminal incident, had stopped going off. "I almost took my beeper in to have it checked," he said (Kennedy et al. 2001, 40).

In November 1996, the *New York Times* published a glowing article about Boston noting that not a single young person under 17 had been murdered in a 16-month period.[1] The sense of astonishment increased as the murder rate continued to plummet. In 1990, more than 150 people were murdered in Boston, including 73 young people. By 1999, the *total* number of citywide murders had plunged to 31.

## Falling Apart

It is an old cliché that failure is an orphan while success has many parents. In Boston, that was certainly true. Success brought with it a new set of challenges, namely how to parcel out the credit.

Other than the notes that Kennedy and his colleagues were taking during the working group meetings, there are few records of what was happening in Boston, and the project itself did not have a single coherent identity. It went by several overlapping names: the Boston Gun Project (the name the police gave to a range of interventions that predated the Harvard researchers), Operation Night Light (the name of the ride-along program for police and probation officers), and Operation Ceasefire (the name coined after Kennedy got involved). And this list doesn't include a range of other names associated with the initiative, including "pulling levers," the Ten Point Coalition (the clergy group), Streetworkers (the street-based outreach workers).

To Kennedy, the debate over who should get credit for Ceasefire unfolded "exactly backwards" (Kennedy 2008). A national consensus developed that Ceasefire *was* effective *before* anyone agreed on what made it effective.

The unconventional nature of the Ceasefire model may have been crucial to its success, but it would prove to be a critical problem limiting its spread. For all the attention the program received, it resisted easy analysis. It would prove even harder to maintain.

According to Kennedy, the pressure was intense and almost immediate. "Within Boston, there became almost a street brawl about what was responsible," he said (Kennedy 2008). Several distinct camps emerged. In one camp were members of the Boston Police Department. In another camp were some of the ministers involved in the Ten Point Coalition, most notably the Reverend Eugene Rivers. A third group was the public health community, which asserted that the presence of street-based outreach workers was the key. In a fourth camp were probation officials who believed that Operation Night Light was responsible for crime declines. Finally, there were the Harvard researchers and their strategy of "pulling levers." University of Wisconsin Professor Michael Scott likened the debate to the fable of the blind men and the elephant: each one touches a different part, and none can agree on what is in front of them. "Depending on whom you talked to, [each camp] would identify a different thing about the intervention that was the cause of its success," he said (Scott 2008).

The stakes were high. Kennedy observed, "It was very clear within Boston that there were careers and reputations and political ground to be won on this" (Kennedy 2008). The working group splintered under the pressure. The most visible casualty was the Ten Point Coalition, itself a loose collaborative of inner-city ministers whose endorsement of Ceasefire had provided important practical support and public legitimacy to the project (Winship and Berrien 1999). The story of the collapse of the Ten Point Coalition is sad to recount, a train wreck that exploded in public view. Inspired by the success of Ceasefire, Ten Point attracted over $10 million in government and foundation grants; but as the group's public profile grew, so too did internal tensions. Unable to manage these tensions, the organization split into three separate and disconnected parts, with each group laying claim to the basic brand name—the Boston Ten Point Coalition, the National Ten Point Coalition, and the International Ten Point Coalition (Braga, Hureau, and Winship 2008). Over time, the disputes took a nasty turn, with the Reverend Jeffrey Brown (who headed the Boston Ten Point Coalition) accusing Rivers of sending henchman his way to threaten to beat him up (McPhee 2006).

According to Anthony Braga, a member of the original Harvard research team, the basic problem confronting the Ten Point Coalitions was "mission drift"—as they attracted more funding, they became more invested in direct service provision, rather than supporting their member congregations and serving as a prophetic voice in the community. The Coalition "went from a movement to an agency," recalled one of its founders (Braga et al. 2008, 11).

Another critical blow to Ceasefire came from the typical forces of failure, most notably the inability to manage the process of succession planning. In 2000, Joyce's successor, Lieutenant Detective Gary French, left for a new position. French's replacement stopped attending the regular working group meetings, and the police returned to more traditional law enforcement tactics. To David Kennedy, this was the moment when Ceasefire, in effect, was "deliberately dismantled." Meanwhile, the murder rate in Boston began to climb, from 31 in 1999 to 75 in 2005, including 39 victims under the age of 25.[2]

Conflict within the police department led to even more chaos. In 2003, Police Commissioner Paul Evans left after serving for almost a decade, and his replacement, Kathleen O'Toole, assigned day-to-day operations to two feuding deputies, Robert Dunford and Paul Joyce. The tensions between the two men, who operated competing antigang initiatives, affected the entire organization. As one observer told the *Boston Globe*, "There are people who are loyal to doing things Dunford's way, and people who are loyal to doing things Paul Joyce's way."[3]

To Teny Gross, an outreach worker who later moved to Providence, Rhode Island, to start an organization inspired by the successes of Ceasefire, the problem was that the working group could not stand up to the pressures of fame. "We were a nimble army, very small and flexible," said Gross. "Suddenly [fame] started getting into people's heads" (Gross 2008). In an op-ed for the *Boston Globe,* Gross was unsparing in his criticism:

> There is no polite way to say it: Boston's regression into its old territorial self has translated directly into death. A decade ago, a young man in Dorchester told me, "You adults are the real gang members, easy to feel slighted, fighting petty beefs, vying for attention and credit." It is the beefs on the streets that get the headlines. But the beefs in the offices and agencies are now equally to blame for what is happening.[4]

## Spreading the Gospel

The collapse of Ceasefire in Boston did not mean that the ideas underlying the program were invalid, of course. In 1997, Kennedy and his Harvard colleagues were invited to Minneapolis, where they created a version of Ceasefire called Hope, Education, Law, and Safety (HEALS). In 1998, the U.S. Department of Justice announced plans to replicate the

Ceasefire model in five cities. The program, known as Strategic Approaches to Community Safety Initiatives, was expanded to 10 sites by 2000. Later, Ceasefire helped inspire an even larger federal government investment, known as Project Safe Neighborhoods, that was implemented in all 94 U.S. Attorney districts around the country.[5]

As criminal justice officials from Philadelphia, Chicago, and Los Angeles began visiting Boston and asking for help and advice, the Ceasefire team learned that the program, which was more a set of provocative ideas than a single coherent model, was difficult to translate.

To Kennedy, Philadelphia was an early example of a city that "completely missed the point" about Ceasefire—an analysis that Streetworker Teny Gross shares. "They brought 25 people [to Boston]," said Gross. "It was heavy duty. [But] when I went to Philadelphia and asked [police] captains, 'Who is killing who?' they just looked at each other. You cannot win a war if you don't know who you are fighting" (Gross 2008).

Chicago offered another example of the challenges of replication. Gary Slutkin, an epidemiologist who had spent over a decade fighting infectious diseases in Africa, decided to apply a public health model to the problem of gang violence in inner-city Chicago. After visiting Boston, he took the Ceasefire name but only adopted the Streetworker part of the model (in which social workers and former gang members are employed to try to quell gang disputes before they turn violent).[6] "The public health people in Chicago just appropriated the brand," said Kennedy. "They just took the name and pasted it onto something completely different" (Kennedy 2008). To add to the confusion, a more faithful adaptation of Boston's Operation Ceasefire, operated by the U.S. Attorney's Office in Chicago, was launched in January 2003. The two projects had nothing to do with one another, according to University of Massachusetts-Amherst Professor Andrew Papachristos (2008), who evaluated the program run by the U.S. Attorney's Office.

In Los Angeles, a Ceasefire replication struggled to get off the ground, hobbled by forces outside the control of the collaborative. According to University of California-Irvine Professor George Tita, a careful marketing strategy carried out by collaborative members in the Boyle Heights neighborhood was abandoned after beleaguered community members urged that a tough law enforcement approach be implemented immediately. As Tita writes, "Events had overtaken the carefully laid plans" (Tita et al. 2005, 14). After federal funding to support the initiative expired, the working group drifted apart. According to reporter Daniel Duane, "If you so much as mention Operation Ceasefire in Los Angeles law enforcement circles, you find a thinly concealed contempt." Los Angeles County Sheriff Lee Baca was openly dismissive of Ceasefire. Ceasefire is "good for a community that has 50 or less murders a year," said Baca. "I would wish that we had that small a problem in L.A." (Duane 2006).

As the Los Angeles experience showed, the combination of factors that laid the groundwork for Ceasefire's success in Boston, such as the dogged determination of frontline practitioners like Joyce to try new things until they got it right, is hard to find. It can't be bottled up and sold. As Tita put it in his blunt assessment of Los Angeles's failures, "The locals saw it as my project and not theirs." His lesson is that "someone other than the research partner has to take ownership" (Tita 2008).

Police officials in Los Angeles were not the only ones skeptical of Ceasefire. To many scholars, the link between Ceasefire and Boston's sudden crime drop was far from a given. Kennedy and his Harvard colleagues were careful to note that they had no definitive proof that Ceasefire had caused the crime drop, although they felt there was strong circumstantial proof that it "worked." They pointed to timing: taking June 1, 1996, as the official start date of the program (around the time when the first forum with members of the Vamp Hill Kings was organized), the number of youth homicides dropped by 63 percent (Braga et al. 2001).

However, when other scholars examined the numbers, they were not as convinced. A key problem was sample size: the relatively small number of youth homicides that occurred in Boston immediately before and during the intervention made it hard for Ceasefire to meet the test of statistical significance. Using a complicated statistical model that incorporates changing crime conditions in 95 U.S. cities, Richard Rosenfeld (whom we met in chapter 1 with the St. Louis Consent to Search program) and his colleagues at the University of St. Louis–Missouri concluded there was about a 10 percent probability that Boston's crime drop had occurred by chance, rather than as a result of the Ceasefire intervention (Rosenfeld, Fornango, and Baumer 2005). Their answer to the question whether Ceasefire works was that they did not know for certain.

This soon became the prevailing wisdom among many scholars. For example, a report prepared for the National Research Council stated that "while there is a strong association between the youth homicide drop and the implementation of Operation Ceasefire, it is very difficult to specify the exact role it [Operation Ceasefire] played in the reduction of youth homicide in Boston" (Wellford et al. 2004, 239).

Kennedy and others involved in Boston found themselves increasingly on the defensive. "I had a conversation with a reporter from the *Boston Globe* soon after things went sour on the streets," Kennedy recalled. "I told the reporter, this is what happened [in Boston], and she said, 'why am I supposed to believe this—[just] because you're saying it?' " For Kennedy, these attacks were deeply discouraging. "I will tell you that people who felt they were central to Ceasefire thought they were being swept away," he said. "Without any clear understanding of what had worked, it was as if Ceasefire never happened," he observed (Kennedy 2008).

Kennedy learned a painful lesson from the Boston experience. It turned out that that it was a lot easier to market Ceasefire to gang members than to the broader policy world.

While there was value in the bracing skepticism that academics and journalists brought to Ceasefire, no one has succeeded in discrediting the strategy. Judging from Boston and subsequent replications (including Minneapolis, Indianapolis, and, more recently, a program in Stockton, California, that was evaluated favorably by Anthony Braga), the weight of the evidence suggests that the model is an effective violence prevention tool after all (Braga 2008).

For all the virtues of careful reflection, it is safe to say that any process that takes more than a decade to reach a tentative, conditional conclusion is not very useful for local practitioners confronting urgent public safety problems. Rather than relentlessly demanding statistical rigor, Professor Robert Weisberg of Stanford University advocates a more relaxed standard for the research community: encouraging the adoption of promising programs that appear to have no significant downside, a standard that Operation Ceasefire certainly passed. If researchers were to follow such a course, Weisberg writes that "officials might feel more motivated to be partners in a series of tinkering, trial-and-harmless-error efforts that might ultimately yield more demonstrably efficacious solutions" (Weisberg 2005, 475).

## Saving Ceasefire

To the broader world, Operation Ceasefire may have seemed like it came out of nowhere; in fact, it was the result of years of groundwork, initiated by Paul Joyce, to address the problem of youth violence in Boston.

What the Harvard researchers added was a way of structuring and marketing some of the strategies that frontline practitioners were already engaged in—what Kennedy and his colleagues call "the power of an outside eye." As Kennedy puts it, the Harvard team was able to "see the significance of an existing practice, determine with the working group its potentially wider application, and articulate the developed strategy to practitioners' own agency leaders" (Kennedy et al. 2001, 21).

By its very nature, the Ceasefire collaborative was a very fragile organism. It involved an alphabet soup of city, state, and federal agencies, each with different missions and organizational cultures. Even after the Harvard researchers came along, it would take over a year for the Ceasefire strategy to take shape. During this period, shocking acts of violence occurred routinely. For example, in what Kennedy and his colleagues call the project's "low point," a member of the Vamp Hill Kings was murdered only minutes after working group members warned the gang member's mother that he was in danger. It takes real commitment to forge on with an unconventional idea in the face of such events.

The irony of the Talmudic parsing over who should get credit for Ceasefire's success is that the project itself depended on a unified vision among a diverse group of constituents on how to target youth violence. To use a scientific analogy, one of the "active ingredients" for Ceasefire's successes was undoubtedly the shared support for the "pulling levers" strategy.

The unraveling of the so-called Boston miracle and the challenges Kennedy faced in trying to export the model have provided him with some hard-earned wisdom. "I [now] see good stuff in criminal justice as fluid and a work in progress," he said (Kennedy 2008). Rather than fold up his tent and quit, Kennedy continues to drum up interest in the "pulling levers" strategy through his writing, lectures, and media appearances.

Kennedy's latest project, an adaptation in High Point, North Carolina, is following the same path blazed by Ceasefire: strong initial results, favorable media attention, and a federal interest in replication. Key to the success of the High Point initiative is the strong support of Police Chief James Fealy, who has worked closely with Kennedy to formulate the strategy. In essence, High Point has offered Kennedy a second chance to test his ideas. He stated, "The big buzz [around Ceasefire] is certainly gone, [but] there's a big audience for High Point right now" (Kennedy 2008). Indeed, in 2009 Kennedy and John Jay College president Jeremy Travis created a new coalition, the National Network for Safe Communities, to spread the High Point/Ceasefire model. Thirty-three cities have signed on to the effort in just the first few months.

While the debate over Ceasefire's impact probably never will be resolved, the project has made an important contribution to the field of criminal justice. The Ceasefire story throws into stark relief several leading causes of failure: namely, the challenges of maintaining a complicated interagency coalition over the long haul, planning for succession of key leaders, managing egos and credit, and overcoming the obstacles of local context in replicating a model program.

For all the negatives, Ceasefire has made a significant contribution to the field of criminal justice, largely because of Kennedy's tenacity. Despite the collapse of Ceasefire in Boston, he has succeeded in building a national network of local innovators who are devoted to moving the underlying ideas forward.

In fact, some of the ideas exemplified by Ceasefire have had a thriving second life in places like Memphis, Chicago, Milwaukee, and Omaha, according to Michigan State University's Ed McGarrell, lead evaluator of the federally funded Project Safe Neighborhoods. For example, McGarrell believes that Project Safe Neighborhoods has proven the value of bringing researchers and law enforcement officials together to jointly investigate and design a response to public safety problems. "Sites that integrated research [and researchers] were more likely to be at the high end of the implementation scale," he said (McGarrell 2008). That was the case even when the problem being investigated was very different from the one Ceasefire focused on originally. In Memphis, for example, a team of researchers and law enforcement personnel focused on the problem of rape and sexual assault. Their data-driven efforts led to a 49 percent reduction citywide in forcible rape (Roehl et al. 2008).

For McGarrell, the value of Ceasefire is that it has helped to introduce a sense of hope into the field of criminal justice. He asserts that "now we have some examples of promising practices. In terms of perspective, it's a sea change" (McGarrell 2008). The years before Operation Ceasefire, after all, had been dominated by a very different emotion, which was resignation. There was a sense among many people, both within and outside criminal justice circles, that crime was essentially like the weather: a problem beyond the reach of human intervention. No matter who deserves the credit or how long the effect lasted, Ceasefire has shown that creative, collaborative work can make a difference, even on some of the meanest streets of Boston.

# The Billion-Dollar Failure
## Parole and the Battle for Reform in California

On a clear morning in the fall of 2008, Chula Vista, California, parole agent Raul Sandoval eyed the man sitting across from him suspiciously. "You know you're not supposed to be living with your mother, right?" he asked. The man (whom we will call Willie, not his real name), nodded sheepishly and shifted uncomfortably in his chair (Sandoval 2008).

"We're going to take a drug test today and I hope for your sake that it comes back clean," said Sandoval, who was dressed comfortably in blue jeans and a baseball cap. Sandoval did not have to explain the rest. As a parole agent, he had the authority to send Willie back to prison for technical violations of parole. The fact that Willie had moved back in with his mother without reporting it was a technical violation, and it alone was enough to get him in serious trouble. A failed drug test would represent a second violation.

Willie was a tough case but hardly unique. He had recently been released from prison after serving a 13-month term for stealing two kegs from a grocery store and tearing a phone out of the wall at his mother's place. His mother agreed to take him in after he left prison, even though that was practically the only place he was not supposed to go. After a few weeks, Willie's mother had called Sandoval, saying she had second thoughts about her decision to let him into the house. She told Sandoval that Willie was moody, unpredictable, and using drugs. To protect her, Sandoval did

61

not tell Willie that his mother had called him; instead, Sandoval claimed that he had found out by happenstance.

Today, Willie was insisting that he was clean and that the drug test would vindicate him. He acknowledged that it was a mistake to move in with his mother without telling Sandoval and said he would arrange to move to his father's place. This did not inspire much confidence. Willie didn't have a job, and it didn't seem like he was trying that hard to find one, either. His main goal in life, as far as Sandoval could tell, was to get high and sponge off of his family.

Sandoval felt that Willie required something more than a verbal warning. However, returning him to prison was probably not the right answer either; it was expensive and, compared to the other parolees he supervised, Willie seemed like a low risk to reoffend. Sandoval's instinct was to get Willie into a structured living situation where he could get some drug treatment and more consistent discipline. He even had a program in mind, called the parolee resource center. It was known as a reliable program, although it was a scarce resource and had to be used judiciously. If Willie got in, that meant he was taking the place of someone else.

Sandoval asked Willie to sit in the lobby until he was ready to administer the drug test. He had one thing he needed to do first. Turning to his computer, Sandoval opened up a program called the Parole Violation Decision Making Instrument (PVDMI). The PVDMI recently had been introduced in Chula Vista and in three other parole units across California; if all went according to plan, it would be rolled out to the rest of the state by the end of 2009.

The PVDMI was designed with one purpose in mind: to help agents make decisions about how best to respond to parole violations. The PVDMI produced a recommendation of how seriously each violation should be treated, depending on the nature of the violation and the risk of the parolee committing a new offense. To determine criminal risk, the PVDMI took into account factors such as age, gender, criminal record, and the number of previous probation or parole revocations.

For technical violations committed by low-risk offenders, the PVDMI would recommend a relatively mild sanction, such as a verbal reprimand or the imposition of a curfew. However, for higher-risk offenders, the PVDMI would recommend something more intensive, such as inpatient drug treatment or a return to prison. The idea was simple: by nudging parole agents to consider the risk of reoffense before making a decision on how to respond to a parole violation, the PVDMI encouraged agents to reserve prison for the riskiest parolees. An agent could override the PVDMI by making a more serious or less serious recommendation than the one produced by the computer. But the agent would have to account for this decision because it would be recorded on a centralized database and subject to review by state administrators.

Sandoval plugged in a few details about Willie's case into the computer, and scrolled down the screen to see what the PVDMI was recommending. He let out a soft murmur of surprise. The PVDMI was telling him that Willie's parole violation warranted the least-intensive response—at most a referral to outpatient drug treatment. In practice, this meant that Sandoval would have to override the PVDMI if he wanted to send Willie to the program he had in mind because, according to the computer, the Parolee Resource Center was only appropriate for parolees in the moderate-response category.

Sandoval's gut instinct told him that Willie needed more than a slap on the wrist if he was going to change his ways. He worried about the message he would be sending if he let Willie get away with a blatant violation of parole. And if Sandoval let Willie walk out of the office and back home, he felt like he might be putting Willie's mother at risk. But the computer was telling him to do it anyway. What, then, was the right thing to do?

All across California, parole agents are making hundreds of decisions like this every day. Willie's transgression represented just one of approximately 187,000 violations that come to the attention of parole agents every year. An examination of these decisions would show that many of them, like Willie's case, involved complicated fact patterns. Viewed from the ground level, there are no easy answers to parole violations, just a lot of grey areas and difficult judgment calls. But if you were to read the flood of op-eds, academic papers, and reports issued about California's correctional system over the past two decades, you would come to a very different conclusion. In their view, the decisions made by Sandoval and the other parole agents in California add up to nothing less than a catastrophic failure.

## Time Is Running Out

In January 2007, the Little Hoover Commission, a nonpartisan oversight commission with members appointed by the governor and the state legislature, released a report with the ominous title, "Solving California's Correctional Crisis: Time Is Running Out." Its conclusion was stark:

> California's correctional system is in a tailspin that threatens public safety and raises the risk of fiscal disaster. The failing correctional system is the largest and

most immediate crisis facing policymakers. For decades, governors and law-makers fearful of appearing soft on crime have failed to muster the political will to address the looming crisis. And now their time has run out. (Little Hoover Commission 2007, i)

The report told a grim story. From 1980 to 2007, California's prison population increased sevenfold to 173,000 prisoners, by far the largest in the country. During the same time period, total correctional spending ballooned from $1 billion a year to $10 billion. Despite these increased expenditures, it was not clear that the people of California were getting a good return on their investment.

The authors of the report were particularly scathing about parole, which they dismissed as a "billion-dollar failure." Almost alone among states, virtually all released prisoners in California are given a three-year parole term, regardless of their criminal history and risk to the community. With the highest number of parolees in the country and caseloads that average about 70 parolees per agent, nearly double the national average, parole agents can barely find the time to meet with parolees, let alone supervise them effectively.

The combination of high caseloads and a lack of rehabilitative options—only about half of state prisoners receive any kind of in-custody education or vocational programming, and services are similarly scarce outside of prison walls—encourage parole agents to recommend incarceration for even minor infractions. "Parole is a system set up to find failure," said Michael Jacobson, author of *Downsizing Prisons: How to Reduce Crime and End Mass Incarceration.* "If what you're interested in is finding failure and putting people back in prison, it's like shooting fish in a barrel."[1]

The process of parolees "churning" in and out of prison for technical violations has driven California's prison population boom for years. As the Little Hoover Commission noted, about 70 percent of California parolees return to prison within a three-year period. In 2006, for example, of the 120,000 people sent to prison in California, 70,000 were sent there for violating parole, either for a new arrest (about 30,000 of the total) or for a technical violation (about 40,000).[2] In other words, every year, tens of thousands of parolees were being sent back to California prisons for violations of the conditions of their parole that did not involve commission of a new crime, such as failing drug tests or moving without telling their parole officer.

What was striking about this practice was that parolees were not being sent back to prison by judges. Instead, their sentences were handed down by civil servants who worked for the Board of Parole Hearings (BPH), in a process known as "backdoor sentencing." In California, as in other states, the standard of proof for dealing with parole violations is much lower than the one used in criminal court. Once a parolee has reached the parole hearing stage, a return to prison is virtually automatic, occurring in about 90 percent of cases. While this practice is not unique to California, the scale of it is. California is the only state in the country that sends more people back to prison from parole than from court, at roughly a 2:1 ratio, the reverse of the national average. (For example, Florida sent 32,253 felons and just 246 parole violators to prison in 2007.)[3]

The ease with which the Board of Parole Hearings could send parolees back to prison created some strange paradoxes. For example, parolees arrested on a new offense were routinely prosecuted through the BPH process rather than through the local courts. While this situation often led to successful prosecutions and eased the financial burden on local jurisdictions (the state bore the cost of parole hearings, including any prehearing incarceration costs), by law the maximum sentence that can be imposed by BPH hearing officers is one year. As a consequence, thousands of serious offenders were being sentenced to short prison terms as parole violators. For example, for the 2003–4 period, BPH returned 246 parolees charged with murder, 1,006 parolees charged with robbery, and 691 parolees charged with rape and serious sexual assault back to prison—all for no more than one year (Grattet, Petersilia, and Lin 2008).

At the high end, then, parolees arrested for serious offenses were getting much shorter sentences than they would have gotten had their cases been prosecuted successfully in criminal court. What was happening to parolees at the lower end of the spectrum also had strange unintended consequences. Any time a parolee was returned to prison for a technical violation, such as failing a drug test, the "clock" on his parole sentence stopped, stretching out the time that person would be on parole supervision and further clogging parole caseloads. The process was known as "doing a life sentence on the installment plan." Once a person was on parole, it was very difficult to get off. The combination of relatively long parole terms, low compliance rates, and the almost automatic process of sending parolees back to prison for violations added up to almost an ironclad guarantee that prison populations would continue to grow. In fact, the state's own internal projections, issued in early 2008, predicted that the prison population would increase by 20,000 in the next few years (Grattet et al. 2008).

Given California's yawning budget crisis, there was broad consensus, including agreement from Republican Governor Arnold Schwarzenegger, that parole needed to be reformed. The answer seemed simple enough: have parole agents stop sending so many parolees back to prison for technical violations. Instead, provide parole agents with a broad range of intermediate sanctions, including drug treatment, mental health counseling, and halfway houses. "There have been more than a dozen reports published since 1990 dealing with the crisis in California's prison system, all of them calling for major reforms," wrote criminologist Joan Petersilia. "They all recommend basically the same things, which include expanded rehabilitation programs, the use of standardized risk assessment tools, and a system of intermediate sanctions for low-risk parole violators" (Petersilia 2008, 341).

To the Little Hoover Commission, this failure to learn from failure—the seemingly willful decision to ignore the recommendations made in previous reports and by previous commissions—was unforgivable. The Commission declared, "The State knows what the answers are. . . . For years, lawmakers and government officials have failed to do their jobs" (Little Hoover Commission 2007). Or, as Petersilia (2008, 341) put it, "Everyone knew what needed to be done, but no one was willing to tackle the problem." In California, criminal justice officials and scholars were nearly unanimous in their assessment of California's parole problem and in the broad outlines of how to solve it. So why hadn't meaningful change happened?

## The End of an Era

To understand the predicament that California is facing, it is helpful to start with the story of Richard McGee and the chi-square, as recounted in Daniel Glaser's *Preparing Convicts for Law-Abiding Lives: The Pioneering Penology of Richard A. McGee* (Glaser 1995).

Trained as an educator, McGee came to California with an impeccable reputation as a correctional reformer. As the first warden of Riker's Island in New York City, he had worked with President Franklin Delano Roosevelt's Works Progress Administration to build a model social service unit at the jail, which included classrooms, a well-stocked library, recreation space, and room for a 30-piece orchestra to rehearse.

McGee became California's first director of corrections, appointed by Governor Warren in 1944. It was a very different time for correctional administrators. For one thing, there was the simple matter of tenure: McGee lasted 23 years, a stark contrast to recent days when the job had changed hands three times in five years. In 1940, California had just over 8,000 prisoners and only a handful of prison facilities. By 1970, the state's population had tripled and so had the number of people in prison. In other words, the rate at which California sent people to prison barely budged under McGee, going from a rate of 118 per 100,000 California residents in 1940 to 125 per 100,000 in 1970. (The rate today is closer to 500.)

McGee and his contemporaries in the field of corrections enjoyed a relatively free hand when it came to making policy. At the time, California had an indeterminate sentencing structure, which gave the parole board wide discretion. For instance, an individual convicted on a robbery charge would be given a sentence of five years to life, with the parole board able to release the offender at any point after five years if it thought he or she had been rehabilitated.[4]

McGee was known as a tireless innovator who respected the value of research and drove his staff to try new things. As the head of corrections, his list of accomplishments was long: he racially integrated prison facilities; introduced a host of in-custody vocational, educational, and treatment programs; built halfway houses for parolees; and engaged in a 17-year effort to persuade the state legislature to reallocate money that was saved in avoided incarceration costs to county probation offices. "It is hard to recapture the excitement of those old days," recalled one close associate. "It was inconceivable that a year could pass without a new experiment . . . a new study, or a new program to train people to do more than they had previously thought possible. . . . It is an exhilarating experience to engage in an enterprise in which all participants are convinced that they are leading the world to great improvements" (Glaser 1995, 39–40).

McGee sought to involve all of his employees in his vision of reform. Prison guards were encouraged to lead group counseling sessions and hold regular meetings with inmates to discuss prison issues, with the goal of making each employee "part of the treatment team." As McGee put it, "Every employee, we don't care what his classification . . . has a responsibility to deal with the emotional and personal problems of the people . . . under his supervision. . . . He has the responsibility of creating an atmosphere within the institution in which people can grow and develop, rather than be oppressed and made more bitter than they were when we got them" (Glaser 1995, 74).

This brings us to the story of the chi-square, a relatively obscure statistical technique. One day McGee surprised a researcher working at a Vacaville prison with a call. "[McGee] said he was making some comparisons and had forgotten how to calculate a chi-square," the researcher recalled. "I refreshed his memory, he thanked me, and I never learned more about the question he sought to answer. But I remained impressed that he was taking this careful empirical approach to hypothesis testing on some management question on which he had to decide, and he was doing the analysis himself" (Glaser 1995, 119–20).

From the vantage point of today's highly politicized crime debates, there is something almost touching about the notion of a state correctional chief having the time to sharpen his pencil and do a chi-square analysis. But it underscores an important point: in McGee's time, correctional policy was thought of as something akin to a science, and criminal justice officials were given wide latitude to set policy.

McGee's time in government ended with the election of Ronald Reagan as California's governor in 1966. Reagan took office advocating a tough-on-crime approach, a harbinger of things to come. The mood of the public had changed. Before long, even liberals were joining in on the act: California's determinate sentencing law, signed by Democratic Governor Jerry Brown in 1977, took away the parole board's authority to release offenders early and tripled the length of parole supervision from one year to three years.

## The Politicization of Crime

With the signing of the 1977 Determinate Sentencing Act, California fundamentally altered its approach to corrections. Gone were the days when individuals like Richard McGee were given relatively free rein to set crime policy. Instead, control of the crime agenda essentially had shifted from "nonaccountable" correctional administrators, judges, and parole boards to "accountable" elected governors, state legislators, and district attorneys.

This was a nationwide trend. By the 1990s, almost all states had abandoned an indeterminate sentencing structure, passing "truth in sentencing" laws that required offenders to serve most, if not all, of their judicially imposed sentences. This shift was the product of an unusual political alliance. Both liberals and conservatives were united in their desire to limit the discretion of officials like McGee. Liberals believed that parole boards made arbitrary and racially biased decisions, while conservatives thought that parole boards were disconnected from reality and full of individuals who naively believed in the rehabilitation of criminals against all evidence. In truth, there were good reasons for both critiques. It turned out that parole boards were pretty lousy at predicting who was safe to release to the community, largely because they relied on an informal, ad hoc decisionmaking process that was rife with biases. A body of research emerged in the 1970s and 1980s with a single theme: giving unfettered discretion to criminal justice officials was a bad idea (Simon 2005).

The result, however, has been a wholesale transfer of authority for criminal justice policy to elected officials, who were only too happy to pass new laws to strengthen the accountability of offenders. According to the Little Hoover Commission, there are more than 1,000 felony sentencing laws and 100 felony sentencing enhancements scattered throughout California's penal code. This "chaotic labyrinth of laws with no cohesive philosophy or strategy" has helped fuel the growth of California's prison population, according to the Commission (Little Hoover 2007). The state has not been able to keep up with the growth: despite building 21 new prison facilities since the 1980s, which cost taxpayers billions of dollars, California prisons are regularly at double or triple their intended capacity.

As the criminologists Frank Zimring, Gordon Hawkins, and Sam Kamin write in their book *Punishment and Democracy,* the key element underlying this paradigm shift in authority was not merely a desire to get tough on crime, but a "decline in the belief of expertise":

> The social authority accorded to criminal justice experts provided insulation between populist sentiments (always punitive) and criminal justice policies at the legislative, administrative, and judicial levels. . . . What has changed in recent years is that the insulation that separated public sentiments and criminal justice decisions has been eaten away. . . . If punishment for crime is not a science, why not view making punishment policy solely as the sort of political act that democratically elected legislators are best suited to perform? (Zimring, Hawkins, and Kamin 2001, 15)

In California, the result has been the sweeping away of nearly every vestige of McGee's legacy, the good with the bad. There was little money for the rehabilitative programs he favored because all the money had to go into building and maintaining prisons. In McGee's time, prison guards volunteered to lead social service groups; now, by necessity, they focused on keeping the growing number of prisoners in line. Perhaps most tellingly, research and experimentation no longer were valued within the department—the Department of Corrections disbanded its research unit in the late 1990s.

## A Changed Job

In tracing the story of California's penal policy from Richard McGee to the 1977 Determinate Sentencing Act to the present day, one theme stands out: the communication breakdown between criminal justice officials and researchers on one hand, and elected officials and the public on the other. It is possible to argue that, during Richard McGee's time, the scales of power tilted too heavily in favor of the former, that criminal justice officials were given too much latitude and were insufficiently responsive to public concerns. Today, the opposite is true, and California has found it almost impossible to claw its way back to equilibrium.

The job of a correctional administrator has changed so much since Richard McGee's time that it is almost unrecognizable. The prestige and respect accorded to individuals like McGee is largely gone. "These are politically volatile, exhausting positions for people," said Thomas Hoffman, California's director of adult parole operations. "This organization has been under the microscope. . . . There's not a day when there isn't some 'hair on fire' disaster" (Hoffman 2008).

There is plenty of blame to go around. Criminal justice officials in California have made decisions that have eroded their own authority. Cutting the research unit may have made short-term fiscal sense, but it deprived McGee's successors of a valuable tool in the fight over correctional policy. In a withering assessment of the state of the department in the early part of this decade, professor Joan Petersilia (2008, 343) wrote that:

California corrections had virtually gotten out of the research business and correctional policy had suffered considerably. Programs were implemented with little regard to rigorous evidence, and, once implemented, few programs were evaluated. Moreover, California officials had become professionally isolated. They seldom hired corrections professionals from outside the state, they did not particulate in the nation's professional organizations, such as the American Correctional Association, nor did they attend professional conferences where they could have learned about the advances in evidence-based practices and the vast literature on "what works" in corrections.

The result, according to Petersilia, was that California was increasingly "out of step with national best practices" (Petersilia 2008, 343).

## The Embedded Criminologist

In February 2004, Keith Carruth, the state undersecretary of corrections, flew to the University of California at Irvine with one mission in mind: to convince professor Joan Petersilia to help the state get out of the fix in which it found itself.

Petersilia was exactly the sort of person that California needed if it was ever going to get back in step with best practices in correctional policy. She had come to the RAND Corporation, a Santa Monica think tank, in the mid-1970s and stayed for two decades. Over time, she grew frustrated with the state's approach to crime and punishment, and began to devote her professional energy to pursuits outside of California. Her initial response to Carruth was blunt: "I told [him] I didn't go to Sacramento (the state capital) anymore," she wrote. Petersilia basically had given up on her home state. "I had spent more than 20 years trying to influence California crime policy . . . and as far I could tell, few of my efforts had made any difference" (Petersilia 2008, 338).

At their meeting in Irvine, Carruth worked hard to overcome Petersilia's resistance, arguing that the recently elected Governor Schwarzenegger was serious about prison reform and offering a seat at the table at the highest levels of state government. It was an effective negotiating strategy. "How could I refuse?" wrote Petersilia. "It was time for me to stop 'talking the talk' about what academics *could* offer policymakers if given the chance, and start 'walking the walk' to see if I could positively contribute" (Petersilia 2008, 339).

The task at hand wasn't an easy one. Criminal justice officials in Richard McGee's time had grown so used to having discretion over crime policy that they were unprepared when it came under attack. If Petersilia and others hoped to reduce the use of incarceration in California, they would have to wage a political fight to reclaim some of the trust and discretion that had been lost over the years.

For the next four years, Petersilia went back and forth between UC Irvine and a series of high-level state government positions and appointments. She served as special advisor to Corrections Secretary Roderick Hickman for over a year before she returned to UC Irvine to create (with state support) the Center for Evidence-Based Corrections. Then she took two extended leaves of absence to chair committees dedicated to correctional reform. She called herself an "embedded" criminologist.

Her record in those four years, even by her own reckoning, was mixed. Petersilia encouraged the department to strengthen its internal capacity to propose, implement, and evaluate needed reforms. For example, in July 2005, at Petersilia's urging, a new Office of Policy, Planning, and Research was created. At the same time, the department was rechristened the California Department of Corrections and Rehabilitation (CDCR), making it one of only three states (along with Ohio and North Dakota) to place rehabilitation in the state agency name. In announcing that the agency would be changing its name, Governor Schwarzenegger said, "It is a new day for Corrections in California. After 30 years of stressing punishment, rehabilitation is back."[5]

Despite this success, it quickly became clear that the politics of crime in California could not be solved by a simple change in vocabulary. In 2004, Secretary Roderick Hickman announced an ambitious plan to reform parole, dubbed the "new parole model," that he estimated would cut the prison population by 15,000 inmates. The reform effort was abandoned the next year, prompted by a three-day crime spree committed by a parolee who had skipped out on an intensive drug treatment program.

In press coverage of the case, it emerged that the guidelines for who was eligible for programming under the new parole model were unclear. (In the typical "gotcha" aftermath of these cases, the press went so far as to name the parole agent involved in the case, as well as his supervisor.) "We really didn't do a very good job on implementation," admitted Hickman, who resigned in February 2005.[6] His replacement lasted only a few months before submitting her resignation. The following April, a federal judge took control of the prison health care system. In May 2006, the state's parole chief was fired after the press discovered that sex offenders were being housed in a hotel near Disneyland. These events led to a host of negative press coverage. The *Washington Post* summed up the flavor of these stories in an article titled "California's Crisis in Prison Systems a Threat to Public."[7]

In May 2007, Governor Schwarzenegger signed the Public Safety and Offender Rehabilitation Services Act, which authorized the construction of 53,000 new prison and jail beds at a cost of $7.4 billion, while at the same time moving the state toward a greater commitment to rehabilitative and reentry services. All 40,000 state prison beds—the remaining 13,000 were allocated to help relieve overcrowding in local jails—were to be reserved for individuals in need of mental health and educational services. At the same time, the act called for the creation of 30 "prison reentry" centers (facilities that house inmates preparing for parole closer to their home communities) to house 16,000 offenders for up to a year. "We're going to build the space so people can learn jobs," said Petersilia at the signing ceremony. "We're going to increase their literacy rate. And we can provide good, solid substance abuse treatment programs."[8] Sixteen months later, however, the Act had failed to get off the ground. After the CDCR made some minor changes to the plan, Republicans and Democrats were unable to come to an agreement on a so-called "cleanup" bill. This left prison reform stuck in legislative limbo.[9]

Another disappointment for the CDCR was that even well thought out reform plans were quietly abandoned without receiving a full test of their effectiveness. For years, Petersilia had urged California to adopt an earned-discharge model that would allow some parolees to be released from parole supervision before their three years were up. By tripling parole terms from one to three years for virtually all released prisoners, the 1977 Determinate Sentencing Act had placed a heavy burden on the California parole system (as well as on taxpayers), with little proven effect. Research showed that the effectiveness of parole supervision decreased after 15 months for most offenders. The point of the earned-discharge model was to free up resources to devote to supervising higher-risk offenders, while dangling the carrot of early parole release as an incentive for low- and moderate-risk parolees to follow parole guidelines (Petersilia 2007). Under the program, eligible parolees who stayed crime free and completed drug treatment and other programs successfully would be released from parole supervision after a six-month period.

In theory, the earned-discharge policy offered a win-win for California because it made parole supervision more effective while limiting the pool of individuals who could be returned to prison for technical parole violations. In the fall of 2007, the CDCR announced with much fanfare its plans to pilot the earned-discharge approach in Orange and San Bernandino counties, confidently predicting that the model would be rolled out statewide by mid-2008.[10] With the CDCR's backing, Petersilia published an op-ed in the *Los Angeles Times* titled "Parole, the Right Way," to explain the program.[11]

However, the earned-discharge program never got off the ground, the victim of California's hothouse political environment. The powerful

California Correctional Peace Officers Association (which represents parole agents and prison guards) came out against it. Although their stated argument was that removing individuals from parole supervision was a threat to public safety, there was speculation that the real reason for their opposition was the fear that parole agents would lose their jobs if parole caseloads were reduced.[12] "[Earned discharge] got so much political attention that we never actually discharged anybody as a consequence of that pilot," said Tom Hoffman (2008).

The consensus among many legislators and experienced officials was that California had reached a breaking point, with needed prison and parole reforms stuck in endless gridlock. "This is a glimpse of the future, of what we have to come, a glimpse of future problems like this one only becoming greater," said Democratic state Senator Mike Machado. "We can't solve big problems."[13] As if more evidence was needed to support this conclusion, in 2009, the state's political establishment was locked in a seemingly futile legal fight to remove a court-appointed federal receiver, J. Clark Kelso, who was calling for $8 billion in new prison health care funding.[14] The state's effort, filed jointly by Governor Schwarzenegger and Attorney General Brown, was summarily rejected by the federal judge overseeing the case in March 2009.[15]

The only ray of hope in California came from an unusual source: the state's fiscal crisis. Faced with a budget deficit of more than $26 billion in 2009, Governor Schwarzenegger and the state legislature had little choice but to swallow hard and cut California's correctional budget by $1.2 billion. To achieve these savings, the corrections department planned to release certain categories of low-risk offenders from prison and place them on house arrest. Under this policy, parolees who commit low-level violations will be monitored using a global positioning system rather than sent back to prison. In a hopeful mood, the editorial board of the *San Francisco Chronicle* assessed the situation this way: "When it comes to California's broken prison system, the budget crisis may have finally left us with no option other than to do the right thing."[16]

## A New Tool

Will the 2009 budget deal represent the dawn of a new era for parole reform in California? History suggests that reformers should be exceedingly cautious about declaring victory. While it is too soon to fully assess the

2009 deal, one thing is certain: the success of any parole reform effort rests as much on the shoulders of parole agents like Raul Sandoval as it does on the shoulders of governors, state legislators, and editorial board writers. All of which brings us back to where we started: the PVDMI pilot in Chula Vista.

As with every other part of California's criminal justice system, the job of a parole agent has changed dramatically in the last few decades. The broad leeway that parole agents were once given has been replaced by multiple layers of reporting and an overwhelming amount of paperwork. (In fact, the most common complaint made by parole agents about the PVDMI pilot in Chula Vista was that it added more paperwork to the mix) (Sandoval 2008).

Despite these changes, parole agents retain a considerable level of discretion. This reality illustrates the truth highlighted by Michael Lipsky in his book *Street-Level Bureaucracy:* policy implementation in the end comes down to the people who implement it (Lipsky 1980). With 187,000 parole violations to deal with every year, every decision made by parole agents like Raul Sandoval has potentially far-reaching implications. For any given case, a recommendation of revocation forwarded to BPH almost guaranteed that a parolee would be returned to prison.

The problem that the PVDMI was created to address was that all the incentives that ruled the day-to-day work life of parole agents in California pointed in the same direction: sending parolees back to prison. For one thing, it was hard work to come up with a community-based alternative sanction for a parole violation. It meant spending a lot of time on the phone trying to get someone into a treatment program and more time following up to see how the parolee was doing. It was much easier to just recommend revocation.

The PVDMI was designed to bring more accountability to the decision-making process. It forced agents to explain their reasoning in cases in which their recommendation was to revoke the parole of a low- or moderate-risk parolee. Also important was the political cover that the PVDMI, in theory, could provide parole agents. Whenever an agent decided to continue someone's parole in the community, there was always the risk that the parolee would go out and commit a horrific crime. And in California, this could be career suicide: a parole agent could wake up one morning and see his or her picture splashed on the front page of the newspaper. As a result, according to San Diego parole administrator Maritza Rodriguez, the prevailing philosophy had been that "custody was safe. We would lock up grandmothers" (Rodriguez 2009). Michael Jacobson, author of *Downsizing Prisons,* put it succinctly, "No parole agent has ever been fired for sending someone to prison for a technical violation" (Jacobson 2010).

By tying decisions to assessments of criminal risk, the department effectively was declaring that, for a large number of parolees, prison was not the optimal response to parole violations. At least in theory, it would be more difficult to hang parole agents out to dry if they could say they were just doing what the PVDMI told them to do.

Finally, the PVDMI was designed to address a counterintuitive problem that had long bedeviled parole administrators. The common assumption was that parole, burdened by impossibly high caseloads, was doing too little to supervise offenders. However, research and experience showed that *too much* supervision had its own risks: the more closely parolees are watched, the easier it is to catch them in a technical violation. The danger of setting parolees up for failure has been well documented, including in a landmark study by Susan Turner and Joan Petersilia.[17]

## Sandoval's Choice

Raul Sandoval's interaction with Willie offered a microcosm of the challenges facing California as it sought to change directions. It was easy enough to say, as the Little Hoover Commission emphatically had, that California needed to stop the revolving door between prison and parole. It was far harder to know at which point the door should be stopped on any individual case.

Sandoval's experience with parolees was telling him that Willie needed more than a verbal reprimand if he was going to stop screwing up, and it was clear that his mother did not want him living with her anymore. But did Willie pose a threat to the public? And what was the nature of that risk anyway? It seemed straightforward enough to recommend that Willie be removed from his mother's home and be placed in a facility where he could be watched carefully and offered some services. But there were dangers to this approach. The most obvious danger was that Willie might not report to the program or might misbehave once he was there. As the violations piled up, Sandoval would be faced with fewer options and an even more difficult choice. In this hypothetical scenario, Willie could end up back in prison even if he did not commit a new crime, all because of the completely defensible actions of his parole agent. The PVDMI forced Sandoval to think twice about going down this road. It also forced him to keep the issue of risk front and center in his deliberations.

After some brief reflection, Sandoval decided that Willie's parole violation was serious enough to warrant overriding the PVDMI. Following procedure, he outlined his argument with his supervisor, who agreed that an assignment to the parolee resource center was a good idea. "He's spent the last six months without a job," she observed, flipping through his file. "What's happening with this guy?"

Sandoval went back to his office and entered the recommendation in the PVDMI, taking care to note the override and clicking through a series of boxes to account for his decision, including the ones labeled "acutely unstable home situation," "demonstrated inability of the offender to support self," and "lack of appropriate program in recommended response level." This took him only a few minutes. As it turned out, the parolee resource center did not have a free bed, so Sandoval told Willie to telephone the center every day at 8 A.M. until a bed became available. In the meantime, Sandoval sternly instructed Willie to follow through on his promise to move out of his mother's house.

Sandoval returned to the mound of paperwork cluttering his desk. He had other parole violations to consider. Under the department's new math, Willie's case would be counted as a success for the moment because he had been kept out of prison. But if the drug test came back negative, or he failed to make a good faith effort to get into the parole resource center, Willie could find himself on a slippery slope toward prison. Willie's fate hung in the balance.

In a sense, the fate of parole reform in California hung in the balance as well. For decades, there has been a broad consensus, at least among criminal justice experts, on what needed to be done to fix California's problems: a renewed commitment to reduce the use of incarceration by changing sentencing laws, reinvesting in rehabilitative programs, and formulating new responses to technical violations of parole. Despite this knowledge, prison admissions and expenditures continued to rise year after year in California.

It is tempting to dismiss California's foibles as the product of the state's unique political culture, which for many years has been hamstrung by the overuse of ballot initiatives that have greatly reduced the flexibility of state decisionmakers as well as the enormous political power wielded by the state correctional officers union. But California's struggles contain broader lessons for those interested in criminal justice innovation. First and foremost, the California story highlights the challenging politics of crime, in which tragic cases often become headline news and efforts to introduce more rational decisionmaking are always susceptible to charges of being soft on crime. Indeed, Republicans in California have already derided the parole reforms contemplated under the 2009 budget deal as "easy" on crime. The horrific allegations against parolee Phillip Garrido—a registered sex offender who, in late 2009, was accused of holding an 11-year old girl hostage for nearly two decades—further threatened the tenuous reform deal.[18]

As of this writing, however, there was encouraging news for advocates of parole reform: legislation passed in the state Assembly and Senate called for the creation of a two-track system for parolees, in which violent offenders (about 40 percent of the total) would remain under parole supervision for three years, while nonviolent offenders (about 60 percent) would be placed on a form of administrative parole (or "parole light," according to Joan Petersilia) after one year of supervision. These changes would also reduce the average caseload of parole agents from 70 to 45 parolees, which would presumably give parole agents more time to supervise higher-risk offenders.[19]

Driven in large part by California's enormous budget crisis, these reforms nonetheless represent a triumph for advocates of parole reform. At the same time, a scathing report released by the California inspector general in November 2009 shows how far parole still has to go. The report, which examined the state's handling of the Phillip Garrido case, contained a number of harsh criticisms of parole, noting "systemic problems which transcend Garrido's case and jeopardize public safety."[20]

Another lesson of the California experience is that, as difficult as it may be to win battles in the state capitol, these victories will take reformers only so far. Almost inevitably, the ultimate success or failure of parole reform rests in the hands of parole officer Raul Sandoval and his colleagues, the street-level bureaucrats who must make thousands of tough judgment calls about individual parolees every year. Without support at both the bottom and the top of the institutional hierarchy, among both line workers and state commissioners, reform efforts are doomed to failure.

5

# Beyond Simple Solutions
## Mastering the Politics of Tragedy in Connecticut

One of the nation's toughest sentencing laws was conceived in 1992, in the backyard of a Fresno, California, photographer whose 18-year-old daughter had just been killed by a parolee. As recounted by journalist Joe Domanick in his book *Cruel Justice: Three Strikes and the Politics of Crime in America's Golden State,* Mike Reynold's proposal was called Three Strikes and You're Out because it required sentences of 25 years to life for two-time felony offenders convicted of a third felony offense. Despite the elegant simplicity of the proposal, Reynold's idea initially failed to gain traction with the state's political establishment. All this changed, however, with the abduction and murder of 12-year-old Polly Klaas in October 1993. Republican Governor Pete Wilson, who was about to begin his campaign for reelection, adopted the Three Strikes idea as his top political priority. Democrats, fearful of being painted as soft on crime, rushed to enact Mike Reynold's proposal into law, word for word (Domanick 2004).

Three Strikes is just one example of a nationwide trend: making criminal justice policy on the basis of exceptional and invariably tragic cases. In fact, it is fair to say that high-profile tragedies like the murder of Polly Klaas have largely dominated the public debate over crime in the past few decades. One sign of this trend is the practice of naming legislation after crime victims, such as Megan's Law, Kendra's Law, and Laura's Law.[1]

The desire to protect the public from dangerous offenders is an understandable and laudable one. However, policymakers have learned the hard way that legislative responses enacted in the cauldron of public outrage can often lead to decidedly negative unintended consequences.

California's Three Strikes law is a good example. In the first few years after the legislation passed, more "third-strike" sentences were imposed as a result of convictions for marijuana possession than for murder, rape, and kidnapping combined (Zimring et al. 2001). Another problem is that the law as written has resulted in similarly situated offenders receiving very different sentences based merely on the order in which their crimes were committed. For example, a felony burglary conviction (which counts as a first strike) followed by a theft conviction (which counts as a second but not a first strike) is treated much more harshly than the reverse. Finally, Three Strikes has helped fuel rapidly rising incarceration rates in California, which, as we saw in the previous chapter, have sent correctional spending spiraling out of control.[2]

The adage "hard cases make bad law" has been put to the test repeatedly in criminal justice. Yet, all too often, criminal justice officials have appeared flat-footed in the midst of crisis, helpless to resist public pressure for sweeping and immediate responses to individual acts of crime. "When you look back, you can see how quickly crime policy can be crafted in response to Willie-Horton-like incidents," said sentencing expert Michael Thompson of the Council of State Governments, referring to the infamous case, memorialized in the 1988 presidential election, in which a Massachusetts prisoner committed armed robbery and rape after escaping from a furlough program (Thompson 2009).

Experienced observers know that the criminal justice system is not really a "system" in any meaningful way. Instead, it is a series of codependent and overlapping agencies (courts, probation, police, prosecutors, parole, public defenders, and others) that exist in a perpetual state of dynamic tension. It is a complicated machine that does not yield easily to simple solutions. For all these reasons, it makes sense to call into question any approach to public safety that purports to be a quick fix.

The likelihood that simple solutions will fail does not reduce the pressure to implement them. The media and public outrage that typically follows tragic events can be enormous. "The press comes to us when something has gone horribly wrong," said Gary Hinzman, the president of the American Probation and Parole Association. "Then the public starts to associate us with that negativity" (Hinzman 2008).

This negative-feedback loop makes criminal justice professionals more likely to be defensive when things truly need to change. "Parole and probation live continuously with what the Federal Emergency Management Agency has . . . experienced in the last few years," said criminologist Todd Clear, referring to the federal government agency much maligned for its ineffective response to Katrina in 2005. As Clear notes, sporadic and intense negative feedback is a recipe for disaster. "People [in criminal justice] learn to be cynical and distrust things that look good. At the same time, they just start to deny it when there are problems" (Clear 2008).

All of the reforms we have discussed thus far—Consent to Search, drug court, Operation Ceasefire, and the PVDMI—have been implemented against this backdrop: a media culture committed to the mantra "if it bleeds, it leads," a political environment that favors simple solutions to complex problems, and a criminal justice community that is understandably risk averse. Is there a way out of this box? If not, is it possible to help policymakers who are committed to rational decisionmaking figure out how to navigate the storm when bad cases happen? Answering those questions requires taking a detour into the turbulent realm of politics to describe an unlikely story of failure avoided.

## A Connecticut Classroom

It is difficult to make a group of college sophomores interested in criminal justice at 8 A.M., but Professor Mike Lawlor is willing to try. Lawlor manages to project an air of modest good humor on a chilly New Haven morning in February 2009, peppering his lecture with joking references to Fenway Park, public indecency, and the movie *American Pie*. He leads a discussion about an incident that occurred the night before, in which a student had emptied out the dorms and caused extensive property damage after pulling a fire alarm. Lawlor asks his class what charges the prosecutor could bring against the student. By the time the class ends, the students are sitting up a bit straighter in their seats.

Lawlor has taught at the University of New Haven for more than a decade. But he is more than an academic. Like Barack Obama when he was at the University of Chicago, Lawlor also serves in the state legislature. It seems like a good deal all around: Lawlor brings a unique perspective to the classroom, and the university lets him organize his schedule around the legislative calendar.

Still, a visitor to the classroom would be hard pressed to identify Lawlor as an elected official, let alone the Democratic cochair of the powerful Connecticut Judiciary Committee. Lawlor is by nature an unassuming person who sees no reason to advertise his status to his students. "I don't like to make too big a deal out of it," he says (Lawlor 2009).

Lawlor may be modest in how he describes himself, but that is not how many in the field see him. For example, Michael Thompson of the Council of State Governments called Lawlor "Lyndon Johnson–esque" for his political savvy and ability to move legislation (Thompson 2009). Lawlor has played a key role in reforming the criminal justice system in Connecticut, convincing Republican Governor Rowland to sign legislation that provides significant funding for parole and prisoner reentry programming. Initially controversial, the bill passed both the state house and senate almost unanimously. By early 2007, Connecticut was known as a national leader in corrections, one of only a few states that could boast it had cut crime and its prison population at the same time.[3]

All of this was placed at risk on July 23, 2007, when two parolees were arrested for a horrific home invasion in Cheshire, Connecticut. That case and the gruesome details that were endlessly publicized by the local and national media threatened to unravel all of Connecticut's painstaking efforts to reduce the use of incarceration. Lawmakers clamored to pass new sentencing laws, including Three Strikes legislation patterned after the California law. After a parolee committed another high-profile crime a few months later, Republican Governor Rell banned the parole of all violent offenders and announced a "zero tolerance" policy for all parole and probation violations. Just a few short months later, the prison population had increased by 1,000, a large number in a relatively small state like Connecticut.

It seemed like Connecticut was fated to follow in the footsteps of states like California, where the politics of crime and the unintended consequences of hastily enacted legislation had led to larger and larger prison populations since the 1970s. But the Connecticut story has a different ending, one that owes a great deal to the behind-the-scenes work of Mike Lawlor.

## A Heinous Crime

The cover of the August 13, 2007, edition of *People* magazine featured a handsome portrait of the Petit family, including William Petit, his wife Jennifer, and their two young daughters, Hayley and Michaela. A prominent local family, the Petits lived in an affluent suburban community in Cheshire, Connecticut. The eldest daughter was set to attend her father's alma mater, Dartmouth. The headline accompanying the photo, however, told a grim story: "Home Invasion Murder: Every Family's Nightmare" (Hewitt 2007).

One night, two men, Steven Hayes and Joshua Komisarjevsky, followed the Petits home from a grocery store. They waited until the middle of the night to break into the house. They knocked William out and dragged him into the basement. They returned upstairs and raped Jennifer and Michaela. At 9 A.M., Hayes drove Jennifer to the local Bank of America branch, where she cashed a $15,000 check to give to the kidnappers. During the transaction, she managed to slip a note to the bank teller, who called the police. By the time the police arrived, however, Hayes and Komisarjevsky had set fire to the house. William Petit managed to escape by crawling out of the basement window, but his wife and two daughters were killed.

The story hit the state with an incredible force. "If this family living in a safe community could be chosen, it could happen to anyone," said Bob Farr, chairperson of the Connecticut Board of Pardons and Paroles (Farr 2008). The details that emerged were not flattering for Connecticut's criminal justice system. Hayes had been in and out of prison for over twenty years. Komisarjevsky had been convicted on 18 separate burglary charges. At his sentencing hearing in 2002, the prosecutor noted Komisarjevsky's disturbing behavior: unlike most burglars, he would enter homes at night when there was a greater likelihood that people were home, and wear night vision goggles so he could watch his victims sleep. The judge who sentenced Komisarjevsky called him a "calculated, cold-blooded predator" (Hewitt 2007). Nonetheless, the parole board had released both of them before they had served their full sentences. What's worse, the two men met at a correctional halfway house where they were roommates.

The calls for Connecticut to adopt more punitive sentencing laws came almost immediately. In mid-August, neighbors of the Petit family organized a rally demanding the passage of Three Strikes legislation just as Mike Reynold had in California. "I don't think it's asking too much to protect those you love by helping this never happen again," said Jessica Ryan, who circulated an online petition in support of Three Strikes.[4] Several state legislators, Democratic and Republican, attended the rally. William Petit endorsed Three Strikes, telling the *New York Times* that "it's almost beyond belief" for someone convicted of multiple violent crimes to "still get out" of prison.[5] In September, Connecticut Senate and House Republicans announced plans to introduce Three Strikes legislation.

The atmosphere got even more heated later that month when a parolee stole a car at knifepoint in Hartford and drove to New York City, where the police shot him. To some, it seemed like Connecticut was in crisis. As Governor Rell put it, the events of the past few months had "destroyed the state's confidence in the criminal justice system."[6] In response, Rell suspended parole for all violent offenders, and ordered that all parolees be returned to prison to serve out the remainder of their term for any parole violation, no matter how minor.[7]

The pressure to impose even more draconian measures and do so quickly was enormous. Mike Thompson recalled traveling with state legislators to a national meeting soon after the Cheshire incident took place. "Everyone was reading the *People* magazine article on the plane," he said. "I could see people crying. I wish people could understand the crushing pressure and emotion that exists in these situations." The successful passage of Three Strikes legislation seemed like a foregone conclusion in Connecticut. Experienced observers were girding themselves for radical changes. "My first thought was that they were going to turn the system upside down," said Thompson (2009).

## Reforming the System

Mike Lawlor was elected to the Connecticut House of Representatives in 1986, at the relatively young age of 29. Fascinated by politics, he had spent a year as a Fulbright scholar in Hungary in 1982 and has maintained a lifelong interest in Cold War history. After graduating from law school, Lawlor worked as a prosecutor in New Haven. A few years later, he decided to quit his job and run for the house seat against the incumbent in the town he had grown up in, East Haven. After an energetic campaign, Lawlor won by a small margin.

Lawlor was elected at a turbulent time for the state. From 1980 to 1986, Connecticut's prison population had doubled to about 6,000, after holding steady at 3,000 for "as long as anyone could remember," according to Lawlor. Just as California had done, in 1981 Connecticut moved from an indeterminate to a determinate sentencing structure, and in the process took away the parole board's authority to release offenders before their sentences were complete. The inevitable result was prison overcrowding, so the state responded by creating "supervised home release," a glorified version of parole that gave wardens of individual prison facilities the right to release inmates to keep their prison population below a predetermined cap.

Supervised home release ended up causing its own set of problems: offenders were routinely serving as little as 10 percent of their sentences before entering the program, which offered minimal supervision at best. In response, the state decided to revive parole in 1990 and eliminate supervised home release, with the stipulation that violent offenders had to spend at least 85 percent of their sentence and nonviolent offenders 50 percent of their sentence behind bars (Coppolo 2008). At the same time, the state embarked on a major prison expansion program that added 10,000 new beds by January 1995.

Lawlor would become an active participant in this process after he became cochair of the Judiciary Committee in 1995. Republican Governor Rowland was elected that same year on a tough-on-crime platform. Despite the construction of several new facilities, prisons in Connecticut were quickly filling beyond capacity. Over the objections of Lawlor and others, in 1999 Governor Rowland signed an $11 million contract to house 500 Connecticut inmates at Wallens Ridge, a prison in Virginia. Two inmates died at Wallens Ridge within a year; under the terms of the contract, Connecticut was liable for any legal damages. In the end, the state paid close to $2 million to settle lawsuits filed by the families of the prisoners.[8]

Despite his prosecutorial background and his passion for victims' rights, Lawlor developed a reputation in Connecticut for his liberal views on crime and justice. In his response to the incidents in Virginia, Lawlor proved that he was a pragmatic politician. In 2003, he worked with Republicans to pass legislation that gave the governor the authorization to send 2,000 more inmates to Virginia (to a facility other than Wallens Ridge) in exchange for a promise to invest over $7 million in new programs designed to limit the return of parolees and probationers to prison for technical violations. The deal was roundly criticized by liberal interest groups and correctional unions, who were furious that inmates could be transferred to a for-profit prison. Despite these criticisms, the bill passed the state senate unanimously and the state house with all but 9 of 152 votes.

It proved to be a tactically brilliant move. The state used the $7 million to hire 96 new probation officers and create pilot programs designed to reduce probation and parole violations. This had the effect of cutting violations by more than 20 percent, which in turn led to a 4 percent reduction in the state's prison population between 2003 and 2006. As a result, Connecticut was able to cancel its prison contract with Virginia, for a savings of over $30 million. "The key is to resist doing the simple thing, dumping a bunch of money into a new prison," Lawlor told a reporter from the *Hartford Courant.*[9]

Connecticut was hailed as a national model in corrections policy. Officials at the Pew Center on the States' Public Safety Performance Project, who singled out Connecticut in a report released in 2007, were quick to credit the actions of the state legislature. "When you go from being one of the highest-growth states to the lowest over a couple of years, that doesn't happen by chance," said Adam Gelb of Pew. "Things in criminal justice tend to move slowly. So when there's that dramatic a change in that short of time, it has to do in large part to the policy change."[10]

## Changing the Focus

Just like everyone else in Connecticut, Mike Lawlor reacted with a mixture of shock and horror when he first heard about the Cheshire crime. His first instinct was to learn as much as possible about the case, so he started calling his law enforcement contacts throughout the state. One fact that stood out was that Joshua Komisarjevsky had served only 5½ years of an 8-year prison sentence, even though he had been convicted on 18 burglary charges. (Komisarjevsky had qualified for parole after serving 50 percent of his sentence because burglary was classified as a nonviolent offense.) The decision of the parole board to release him was sure to be a target of criticism, and Lawlor wanted to find out what had gone into the board's deliberations (Lawlor 2009).

Lawlor knew something that only a few people in Connecticut were aware of at the time. In 1997, he had helped pass a law requiring prosecutors to deliver sentencing hearing transcripts to the parole board. The idea was to make sure the board knew all the key details about a case, including statements made by the judge, prosecutor, defense attorney, and victims. "We wanted to avoid a situation [in which] victims in the future would feel like their views weren't being heard," said Lawlor. However, Lawlor knew that prosecutors were routinely ignoring the law, largely because the state's information technology systems were so primitive. Transcripts (which routinely went into hundreds of pages) were too large to be sent as e-mail attachments, which meant they had to be photocopied and mailed, transforming what could have been a simple act into an administrative hassle.

Lawlor was not surprised to discover that prosecutors had not sent the Komisarjevsky transcript to the parole board. So, with the help of a friend, Lawlor got a copy of it. It was a doozy. "It went on for page after page with his defense attorney, the prosecutor, and the judge [talking] about how dangerous this kid is," said Lawlor (2009). It was clear that Komisarjevsky was a deeply troubled human being. He had been arrested only once but had immediately confessed to 17 other burglaries, which the police found credible given his eerie ability to describe, in precise detail, what he had stolen. In and out of foster care, he had been raped repeatedly and first came to the attention of the authorities as a juvenile when he burned down a gas station.

This was what the parole board would have known if it had looked at the transcript of the sentencing hearing. Instead, it had relied on reports of his spotless prison record—Komisarjevsky was known as a model prisoner—along with the fact that he had a job and a home waiting for him upon his release. Based on this incomplete picture, Komisarjevsky seemed like a reasonable risk to the board.

Lawlor made the sentencing transcript public a few days after the Cheshire incident took place, demanding to know why the parole board had not had access to the information. (He had raised the issue many times in the past with prosecutors, to no avail.) His message to the press was simple: "If you're looking for an outrage, this is it." The story of the missing transcript dominated headlines for days. Michael Thompson recalled that "[Lawlor] spent an incredible amount of time on the phone with reporters, patiently walking them through the story" (Thompson 2009). It was painstaking work, in part because of changes in the newspaper industry: many of the veterans on the crime beat had been replaced by younger, cheaper, and less-informed reporters, and Lawlor had to take more time to make sure they understood the basics of Connecticut law.

Lawlor's hard work paid off, as the controversy over the transcript helped shift the terms of the debate. By giving the press a specific, tangible issue to focus on, he managed to draw some attention away from the calls for Three Strikes legislation. "It became clear to me that the real problem was that people making the decisions didn't have the information they needed," Lawlor said (2009). Moreover, in his conversations with the press, Lawlor was careful to point out that Komisarjevsky would not have been prosecutable under a Three Strikes law because all 18 of his convictions had occurred as the result of a single guilty plea. In addition, prosecutors in the 2002 case against Komisarjevsky had the authority to seek a life sentence against him but chose instead to accept a plea bargain. The clear implication was that Three Strikes would not have prevented the Cheshire crime from happening.

## Confronting Consequences

In late July 2007, three days after the Cheshire murders, Governor Rell announced the formation of a task force, composed of top state officials, to perform a "top-to-bottom assessment of all the procedures and processes involved in the charging, sentencing, and releasing of those convicted of crimes in Connecticut." At the same time, the Democratic speaker of the Connecticut House asked the Judiciary Committee to hold hearings on improvements to the state's criminal justice system, to be cochaired by Lawlor.

This gave officials in Connecticut some breathing space, but not much: the House and Senate were next scheduled to convene in September. On September 6, Republicans, in the House and Senate held a joint press conference announcing their proposed Three Strikes legislation and demanding that the special session be opened to allow for its passage. Lawlor scrambled to respond, fearing that if the special session were opened to discuss the Three Strikes legislation, it would be impossible to keep it from being enacted. Acting quickly, Lawlor organized a meeting of the Judiciary Committee. He called Michael Thompson to help identify credible, non-ideological witnesses who could raise questions about the effectiveness of Three Strikes laws and help make the case that more study was needed. Among them were James Fox, a California prosecutor who was the president of the National District Attorneys Association, and Michael Jacobson, the former commissioner of corrections under New York City Mayor Giuliani. Their message was that Three Strikes was no panacea. "The testimony was very neutral—they had no axes to grind," said Lawlor. "I could see [that] the Republicans [on the Committee] were upset, because they thought I would bring in people from the ACLU" (Lawlor 2009).

To Lawlor and other experienced criminal justice policymakers, the danger with a hastily written Three Strikes law was that it would distract public and legislative attention from the kind of structural reform that

Connecticut desperately needed, including improvements in information-sharing across law enforcement agencies. "Our information technology system was just backwards," said Connecticut Chief State Attorney Kevin Kane. "From the police officer on the street to [officials] at the Board of Parole and Pardons, decisionmakers weren't getting the information they needed." Cheshire had exposed that key gap, but, as Kane put it, information technology was hardly a "sexy" issue. Kane, appointed by Republican Governor Rell in 2006, was neutral on Three Strikes. He believed it would have little practical effect on Connecticut—in his opinion, the penalties already on the books in the state were high enough. "My concern with Three Strikes was that had the legislature adopted it, they and the public would think we had solved all our problems," Kane said (Kane 2009).

Lawlor's efforts to delay the introduction of Three Strikes legislation paid off. On a party-line basis, both chambers voted on September 20 against opening up the special session to deal with criminal justice reform issues, arguing that the state needed more time to gather the facts and come up with solutions. It was a small but crucial victory for the cause of deliberation and rational policymaking.

In a sign of the key role that luck and timing can sometimes play in these types of situations, on the very next day, a Connecticut parolee was shot and killed by a police officer in New York City after stealing a car at knifepoint. Had the incident occurred only a few days earlier, it would have been much harder for Democrats to appeal for more time.

Lawlor had succeeded in delaying a vote on the Three Strikes legislation, but supporters of the idea were sure to put the issue back on the table when the legislature reconvened in January. Instead of directly taking on the Three Strikes proposal, he ordered the Judiciary Committee to begin planning for a massive expansion of the state's prison system. The goal was to confront supporters of Three Strikes laws with the potential implications of what they were proposing. Lawlor asked the Department of Corrections to submit a plan for building new prison capacity within Connecticut, on the premise that it would take at least four years for it to move through the regulatory and construction process. According to the estimates that Lawlor received, two new prisons would cost $260 million to build and at least $45 million a year to operate, and the only site that could accommodate the facilities was in a town immediately next to Cheshire. As Lawlor noted, there was one other option: to spend millions to renovate a mothballed, 400-bed wing of one of

Connecticut's four existing prison facilities, which, as it happens, was located in Cheshire.

Instead of an abstract debate, Lawlor was forcing the rest of the legislature to think through the fiscal consequences of expanding the state's prison population and the political consequences of where to locate new prisons. It was a risky strategy. It left Republicans with the option of calling Lawlor's bluff and voting to spend the money to build new prisons. But it worked. In November, Governor Rell publicly denounced building new prisons, noting that "when we talk about siting a new [prison] facility, there are few people who want us to look into their towns." She concluded, "Before you go down that road [of building more prisons], you have to look at other alternatives first."[11]

## Lawlor's Triumph

In January 2008, a veritable blizzard of proposals greeted legislators as they gathered for a session devoted to criminal justice reform. The Judiciary Committee produced 15 recommendations, while Governor Rell's task force, the caucuses of both parties, and Governor Rell herself added dozens more.

There were some broad areas of agreement among the various proposals, which were packaged into legislation proposed by Governor Rell and passed into law in late January. Interestingly enough, most of the measures involved efforts to strengthen the capacity of the state's criminal justice system, rather than enhanced sentencing penalties; in fact, Governor Rell's task force did not include a Three Strikes proposal in its list of recommendations.

The main provision of the new legislation was the establishment of the Connecticut Criminal Justice Information System, a new agency charged with creating a centralized database for sharing data across 15 law enforcement agencies.[12] The legislation also required that appointments to the Board of Pardons and Paroles be made on a full-time rather than a part-time basis. With the exception of a change to the penal code that created a new crime for home invasion and increased penalties for repeat felony offenders, Connecticut was signaling its interest in technocratic and carefully thought-out reform.

However, under pressure from members of her party, Rell allowed Republicans to submit a Three Strikes amendment to her proposal.

Democrats, who held the majority in each chamber, stood firm and sent the amendment down to defeat. On January 25, Governor Rell signed the legislation into law and two days later lifted her four-month ban on parole.

Buoyed by their success in defeating Three Strikes legislation and concerned about prison overcrowding, the Democrats returned a few months later with a package of proposals aimed at strengthening the capacity of parole and probation to supervise offenders in the community. The legislation, which was signed into law on April 24, included $10 million in prisoner reentry funding, including money specifically set aside for housing, mental health, and drug treatment services. Passed nine months after Cheshire, the legislation was a triumph for Lawlor and his legislative allies. "This is a huge day for public safety and for the rule of law in Connecticut," said Senate Democratic President Donald E. Williams, Jr. "We're not waiting for a third strike to get tough on crime. . . . [With] the $10 million that we are dedicating for . . . more treatment beds and re-entry programs, . . . the people of Connecticut can see that we are committed to real and meaningful public safety changes and are not simply resorting to bumper-sticker slogans."[13]

## One Last Gasp

Despite their inability to pass Three Strikes legislation, some Connecticut Republicans thought that it could be used as a campaign issue in the 2008 elections. The hope was that Republicans running against incumbent candidates could attract public attention and votes by supporting Three Strikes laws. In September 2008, Republican Senator Sam Caliguiri created the Three Strikes Now Coalition, with William Petit, Jr. and his sister Johanna Petit-Chapman as honorary cochairs. "We believe there's a massive amount of grassroots support on this issue," Caligiuri said at the press conference announcing the formation of the coalition. "Campaigns are the time to have these public policy discussions."[14]

The coalition's first act was to mail pledge cards to legislative candidates of both parties. All told, 58 candidates, including 7 Democrats, signed pledge cards. William Petit began crisscrossing the state with Caliguiri, appearing at press conferences and candidate forums, including one held in Mike Lawlor's district.

It quickly became clear that the Three Strikes proposal was not generating the kind of attention and political momentum that its backers desired. For one thing, 2008 was a very good year for Democrats, with 61 percent of state voters pulling the lever for presidential candidate Obama. Secondly, much of the urgency that initially generated the Three Strikes idea had faded. While some of this can be attributed to the simple passage of time, another factor was Lawlor's success in arguing that a Three Strikes law would not have prevented the Cheshire tragedy. That was clear in some of the language used by the Petit family; for example, in September, even Johanna Petit-Chapman acknowledged that "a Three Strikes law would not have prevented that heinous crime from happening."[15]

Election Day ended in disaster for advocates of a Three Strikes law. All told, 64 percent of the candidates who signed the pledge card lost, including 8 of 15 senate candidates and 29 of 43 house candidates. Perhaps most notably, Republican incumbent Al Adinolfi, a neighbor of the Petit family and a strong supporter of a Three Strikes law, lost a close election to Democratic challenger Elizabeth Esty in what press accounts called "one of the few upsets of the night."[16] Along with Caliguiri, Adinolfi was perhaps the candidate most identified with the Three Strikes proposal. According to Lawlor (2009), it was the "single best indication of the success of our political strategy."

## Postpartisan Criminal Justice

What is most remarkable about the 15-month period between the Cheshire slayings and the 2008 elections is what did *not* happen. Unlike California, Connecticut was able to weather the political and media firestorm that typically surrounds high-profile crime tragedies. The state ended up choosing analysis and incremental reform over emotional decisionmaking and sweeping change.

Connecticut is a striking exception to the nationwide pattern of setting crime policy in reaction to the latest scandal. From 1981 until the Cheshire crime, Connecticut had gone through several significant shifts in sentencing policy that were driven by the same formula: an outrageous crime followed by negative press attention and widespread public anger, followed by major legislative change. At first, the Cheshire incident appeared to set the stage for yet another radical change. "The press got into this kind of feeding frenzy in which every crime committed (after Cheshire) would get blamed on the system," said Bob Farr, chairman of the Connecticut Board of Pardons and Paroles. Farr recalled the news story about a parolee who went to visit his girlfriend, only to find her dead. After an investigation, it was confirmed that she had died of natural causes. "The headline of the *Hartford Courant* was 'Parolee Escapes Murder Charge,' " said Farr. "But there was no murder!" (Farr 2008).

"People who resist major changes to crime policy [following a tragedy] will often say, 'this is an isolated incident,' " observed Michael Thompson. "What Mike [Lawlor] said instead was, 'I want to know what caused this and I want to fix it.' It's a much better argument politically, and he grasped that instinctively" (Thompson 2009). Lawlor's strategy was straight out of politics 101: it is always better to play offense than defense. In the case of Cheshire, Lawlor identified a tangible problem that could be addressed via legislation—that is, the failure of prosecutors to deliver the Komisarjevsky sentencing transcript to the parole board. "The public expects that something will be done," said Lawlor, "and you need to be able to react" (Lawlor 2009).

But Lawlor took it a step further. By forcing discussion about the costs and consequences of Three Strikes laws, such as the need to build new prisons, rather than merely opposing the idea on ideological grounds, he was able to introduce a note of realism to the debate. In formulating criminal justice policy, Connecticut and other states rarely have been forced to consider the likely consequences of their decisions, which only has encouraged the natural instinct of many politicians to adopt simple solutions to crime. Lawlor's insight was to use the political process as a means of forcing a more thoughtful debate about the pros and cons of Three Strikes legislation and to couch that discussion in the language of real-life pragmatic concerns rather than in moral terms. His success is a striking rejoinder to those critics who worry that effective politics and smart policy will always be pitted against one another when it comes to criminal justice.

Even more remarkably, by setting the terms of the debate, Lawlor and his allies were able to prod Connecticut into addressing structural problems that under ordinary circumstances would have been ignored. Employing the old adage "never let a crisis go to waste," they passed legislation that included significant investments in information technology. "We wouldn't have gotten the technology fix without Cheshire," said Connecticut State Attorney Kevin Kane (2009).

Lawlor's success was rooted in his nonideological approach to criminal justice. Lawlor has been in the legislature for more than two decades and has developed a deep expertise in criminal justice issues. "Mike's a real policy wonk," said Michael Thompson. "He doesn't draw too much attention to himself" (Thompson 2009). His low-key, behind-the-scenes leadership was crucial in building a solid foundation of political support for alternatives to incarceration, a foundation that helped Connecticut weather the Cheshire storm.

Instead of leading a passionate crusade against Three Strikes proposals that was steeped in the vocabulary of social justice, Lawlor took a different approach by stepping back and pointing out some of the fiscal implications of the proposal. "It's good to be boring," said Lawlor. "Progressive reformers are too easily painted as soft on crime. It's better not to be viewed as a passionate advocate." To Lawlor, the lesson is that "most of this stuff is not ideological. I've seen all these political battles [over crime policy], but when you talk to people on the front line, almost all of them agree on what the problems are within the system" (Lawlor 2009).

To be sure, party politics played a role in the Three Strikes debate. At several key moments, Democrats were able to vote down Three Strikes legislation by keeping their caucus together. That kind of party discipline is easier to achieve in a traditionally liberal state like Connecticut and in a favorable election year for Democrats. Yet resistance to Three Strikes laws went deeper than mere partisan politics. "I don't see this as a Republican-Democrat kind of thing," said Connecticut Attorney General Kevin Kane. "There was a significant core group of people who recognized the problems within the system." Ultimately, in response to the Cheshire murders, Connecticut decided to roll up its sleeves and get serious about criminal justice reform, which took support from a wide range of policymakers and criminal justice officials. "People get the [mistaken] idea that Three Strikes is a fix that would make the public safe," said Kane (2009). "We recognized that something else had to be done that was more important than [passing] a Three Strikes law."

Evidence suggests that the policy moves Connecticut made in the aftermath of the Cheshire crime have paid off. Between February 2008 and January 2009, the state shed almost all of the prisoners who had been added because of Governor Rell's ban on parole. In fact, the state's prison population in January 2009 was almost indistinguishable from what it was on July 23, 2007, the day the Cheshire incident took place. The state's own projections are that "the prison population is expected to remain stable or realize a modest decline over the next three years" (Connecticut Office of Policy and Management 2009, 3). At the same time, Connecticut has moved forward on technology reform by hiring the first executive director of the Connecticut Criminal Justice Information System in November 2008. According to Kane, the state should see the fruits of these efforts within a few years. "It's going to change how we do business," said Kane (2009).

While the inner workings of the Connecticut state legislature are a world apart from the daily challenges that confront the typical police chief, presiding judge, or probation official wrestling with a seemingly intractable public safety problem at the ground level, these players are subject to many of the same pressures that confronted Connecticut lawmakers in the aftermath of Cheshire. From Lawlor's mastery of the politics of crime, reformers can learn several lessons, among them the value of using nonideological language, the importance of developing an effective media strategy, and the need to avoid appearing defensive when things go wrong.

As for Lawlor, the routines of life have not changed much. Each fall, he teaches criminal justice to a new class. As the years pass, very few of his students will know that Lawlor helped to shepherd Connecticut through some of the most difficult criminal justice challenges imaginable.

# 6

# Defining Failure

Frank Kolarik could not have predicted that he would go from jumping out of airplanes as part of the U.S. Army's 82nd Airborne Division to teaching fifth graders about the dangers of drug abuse at Wampus Elementary School.

After participating in the invasion of Panama, which led to the ousting of General Manuel Noriega in 1989, Kolarik hurt his knee and finished his stint with the U.S. Army in the criminal investigations unit. Working as a police officer seemed like a natural next step, so Kolarik found a job with the New Castle Police Department, located in an affluent suburb 30 miles north of New York City.

It was at the police academy that Kolarik found his calling. He heard a presentation about the Drug Abuse Resistance Education (D.A.R.E.) program, which uses police officers to provide educational sessions about drugs and drug abuse to elementary school students.[1] "The program looked impressive, and I mentioned to the chief that I was interested in participating," Kolarik (2008) recalls. He got his chance two years later, when the department's previous D.A.R.E. instructor moved on. That's how Kolarik ended up spending a large part of the past 12 years at Wampus Elementary, one of 15,000 police officers nationwide who participate as D.A.R.E. instructors certified by the national nonprofit organization D.A.R.E. America.

It doesn't take long to understand why Kolarik enjoys his work at Wampus. He's a natural, with an ease and comfort around young people that is characteristic of any good educator. The kids love him, greeting him with happy cries of "Officer Frank!" as he walks down the hallways. And after 12 years of coming to the school, he's on a first-name basis with everyone in the building, including the school's principal, Barbara Topiol.

On a fall morning in 2008, Kolarik is teaching three fifth-grade classes, one after another in short 45-minute bursts, with a quick break between the second and third class. At 11:55 A.M., after the students have finished their lunch, settled into their seats, and pulled out their colorful D.A.R.E. workbooks, Kolarik begins by briskly answering a few questions about his police work ("Have you ever shot anyone?" "Have you ever been in a car chase?"). Then he moves on to the main lesson of the day, which involves getting the students to think about how peer pressure can influence decisions about experimenting with cigarettes, which D.A.R.E. sees as a gateway to future drug use.

Kolarik uses a simple exercise to drive the point home, asking the students to guess the percentage of eighth graders who have smoked a cigarette in the past 30 days and then giving them a chance to adjust their guesses after they hear what their classmates have to say. Most of the initial guesses are between 40 and 50 percent, and the kids who give lower estimates adjust their answers upward when given the opportunity. The big "aha" moment comes when Kolarik reveals that the answer is only 7 percent, an announcement that causes some of the more competitive students to let out a squeal of disbelief. He asks the students to reflect on the role peer pressure played in how they revised their guesses, as well as how the higher estimates might influence them to try a cigarette themselves. "What you think other people are doing makes a difference in what you do yourself," he tells them.

In each class, Kolarik methodically goes through a formal curriculum created by the D.A.R.E. program. By the end of the week, Kolarik will be back at Wampus two more times, teaching the same lesson to ten different classes. Between October and April, he will be at the school three times a week, and by Christmas, he will know the names of every one of the 250 fifth graders by heart. As the police department's youth officer, responsible for investigating crimes involving young people, Kolarik sees D.A.R.E. as an essential part of his job, an opportunity to get to know kids living in the community on a positive basis. "I like doing this work," Kolarik says (2008).

Overall, D.A.R.E. seems like a good deal for everyone involved. The kids seem to like Kolarik and look forward to seeing him in the classroom. The school benefits because of the relationship it has built with the police department. Moreover, Kolarik enjoys the work.

There's only one problem. According to a long line of research, D.A.R.E. is a failure.

Among criminal justice programs, D.A.R.E. is unique in terms of the enmity and controversy it has generated. On the one hand, the scrutiny that D.A.R.E. has received should not come as a surprise: since 1983, when it was launched in Los Angeles by Police Chief Darryl Gates, it has grown into the nation's largest and most popular program of its kind, making it a natural target for scholarly research (Rosenbaum 2007). D.A.R.E. is active in 75 percent of school districts nationwide, according to D.A.R.E. America Executive Director Frank Pegueros (2008). Success on this scale always draws critics.

Yet the level of criticism that D.A.R.E. has attracted cannot be explained by the size of the program alone. Some of the criticism most likely is based on ideology: launched at a time when youth drug use was considered an urgent national problem, D.A.R.E. will probably always be linked to Nancy Reagan's campaign to "just say no" to drugs, a slogan that today seems like a relic from another era.

But much of the criticism of D.A.R.E. is based not on politics but on data. The scholarly record on D.A.R.E. is clear. In the past 15 years, no fewer than 30 studies have taken aim at the idea that D.A.R.E. effectively prevents drug use among young people.[2] One intensive six-year study coauthored by Dennis P. Rosenbaum of the University of Illinois at Chicago even found that the program *slightly increased* drug use by suburban teens, leading him to recommend that government agencies and local jurisdictions "just say no to D.A.R.E." (Rosenbaum 2007).

Today, the mere mention of D.A.R.E. produces an angry response from many criminologists. "Why would you think D.A.R.E. works in the first place?" asks Frank Cullen, a professor at the University of Cincinnati. "All that wasted time and money . . . could have been spent on a more effective program" (Cullen 2008).

To some observers, D.A.R.E. (along with boot camps and "scared straight" programs) has become a symbol of how difficult it is to kill failed initiatives. By calling on the support of local police chiefs and school administrators, the program has become a potent political force on both the local and national levels. For example, every year for the past 18 years, four consecutive presidents have designated a day in April as National D.A.R.E. Day. To Rosenbaum, support for D.A.R.E. is "like an addiction. It becomes hard to challenge programs like D.A.R.E. as they become routine" (Rosenbaum 2008).

To its critics then, D.A.R.E. is a cautionary tale of how criminal justice programs can live on despite ample evidence they are failures, while more promising approaches are left unfunded. Yet the D.A.R.E. story is more complicated than it appears at first glance. As it turns out, defining failure is much more difficult than it seems.

## A Contentious Relationship

By the time Frank Kolarik first heard about D.A.R.E. in 1994, the hostility and suspicion that have characterized the relationship between the program and the scholarly community had already begun. Much, although by no means all, of this hostility can be laid at the feet of D.A.R.E.'s first national leader, Glenn Levant.

In 1983, Levant was a commander in the Los Angeles Police Department when Police Chief Darryl Gates hit on the idea of sending police officers into the classroom to educate young people about drugs. The program proved to be an immediate hit, and other schools began asking Gates for help. To raise money, in 1984 Levant helped organize the Los Angeles Police Crime Prevention Advisory Council, which later evolved into D.A.R.E. California. A few years later, D.A.R.E. America was established when he landed a $140,000 grant from the U.S. Department of Justice. By 1992, D.A.R.E. was receiving $10 million each year through congressional earmarks.

D.A.R.E. grew quickly, largely because of its success in generating federal support. After only a decade of existence, the program was reaching 5 million students in 60 percent of the school districts across the country, according to the *USA Today*.[3]

Early research on D.A.R.E., however, raised questions about the program's effectiveness. With support from the Department of Justice, the Research Triangle Institute conducted the first national study of D.A.R.E. Preliminary results from the study, which were released in 1993, showed that the program's long-term impact on youth drug use was negligible. D.A.R.E. America publicly criticized the report and pressured the Department of Justice not to release it (Boyle 2001).

This set the pattern for the better part of a decade, with Glenn Levant, the founding president of D.A.R.E. America, regularly blasting researchers, and researchers blasting back. Levant's scorched earth policy—he was described by journalist Patrick Boyle as someone who "goes after foes like a blunt instrument"—helped poison the waters with many in the research community, who saw his attacks as unfair and unwarranted (Boyle 2001).

The controversy over D.A.R.E. reached a fever pitch after the release of a 1998 report by Dennis P. Rosenbaum and Gordon S. Hanson, which followed 1,798 urban, suburban, and rural sixth graders who had participated in the D.A.R.E. program. The research confirmed earlier findings that program benefits, such as educating young people about drugs, improving attitudes about the police, and giving young people the confidence to resist illegal drug use, wore off within one or two years. What really got people's attention, however, was the report's finding that D.A.R.E. was associated with an *increased* level (3 to 5 percentage points) of drug use by suburban youth (Rosenbaum and Hanson 1998).

According to Rosenbaum, D.A.R.E. America played hardball to shape how the report's findings were covered in the national press. "Behind the scenes, they had used high-powered lawyers to sue or threaten to sue people who criticized the D.A.R.E. program, arguing that reporters, producers, and researchers were making false statements," wrote Rosenbaum. "Reputations and careers were ruined" (Rosenbaum 2007). In practice, Levant's strategy appears not to have worked: the report by Rosenbaum and Hanson received widespread national coverage, including numerous newspaper articles and a segment on NBC's *Dateline*.

With the benefit of hindsight, D.A.R.E. America staff and supporters now admit that the approach taken by Levant was heavy-handed and counterproductive. One prominent D.A.R.E. supporter called it a "bunker mentality" (Boyle 2001). "Glenn was very vocal in his utter disdain for most of the researchers," recalled Jim McGiveney, a D.A.R.E. America regional director. "It was almost [like] going back to the 1950s in terms of [Levant] accusing researchers of being communists who were going to tear the fabric of society apart" (McGiveney 2008). His attitude toward researchers could be summed up by a quote he gave to USA Today: "Scientists tell you that bumblebees can't fly, but we know better."[4] McGiveney's take is that Levant, who had helped grow D.A.R.E. from humble origins, simply took criticism too personally. "I can understand why Glenn was so defensive," McGiveney said, "because D.A.R.E. was his baby" (McGiveney 2008).

For all his anger and energy, Levant could not stop the tide. Seattle Police Chief Norm Stamper decided to drop the program in 1996, calling it an "enormous failure." His decision attracted national media attention.[5] Even more ominously for D.A.R.E., the criticism was reaching its allies in Congress. "You'd walk into a congressman's office, and they'd meet you at the door with printouts of studies saying that D.A.R.E. didn't work," said D.A.R.E.'s McGiveney. "That was very tough to overcome" (McGiveney 2008). In 1998, a House Appropriations subcommittee took the unusual step of calling for D.A.R.E. America to revise its curriculum.

With tempers running high, the U.S. Department of Justice intervened. At the request of D.A.R.E, in May 1998, it convened a meeting among a small group of researchers and D.A.R.E. America administrators. To the relief of many, Levant did not attend. Nonetheless, it was a tense meeting. As researcher Richard Clayton recalled, "there was blood on the floor" before participants broke for lunch. Early in the day, Dennis Rosenbaum challenged D.A.R.E. America to defend its decision to highlight a positive study on its web site that, in the words of Richard Clayton, "wouldn't get a C minus in an undergraduate class." He also demanded that D.A.R.E. America delete from its web site some references to his study that he thought were misleading. After some back and forth, D.A.R.E. America agreed, an important first step (Boyle 2001).

In Washington and at subsequent meetings, D.A.R.E. America showed a willingness to make peace with the research community. This made an impression on the Robert Wood Johnson Foundation, which was interested in making an investment in youth drug prevention initiatives. Although the foundation was aware of the critical research on D.A.R.E., it also noted some of the organization's achievements that were often overlooked in the growing controversy over D.A.R.E.'s long-term impacts. Most notably, the organization had built an impressive infrastructure. Through state and regional chapters, D.A.R.E. was training over 1,000 police officers every year. It was "one of the best training systems we had seen," according to the foundation's vice president, Nancy Kaufmann (Boyle 2001). In addition, with programs in school districts across the country, D.A.R.E. America had an unmatched network of local supporters. Rather than trying to replace D.A.R.E. with something else, the executives at Robert Wood Johnson thought it made sense to retool it (Boyle 2001).

Robert Wood Johnson agreed to commit $14 million to D.A.R.E. over a five-year period, a stunning act given the public battering the program was experiencing. Rather than invest directly in D.A.R.E., Robert Wood Johnson decided to have its funds administered by Zili Sloboda at the University of Akron. Sloboda had formerly worked at the National Institute on Drug Abuse and was well known within the drug prevention community. Her job was to create and evaluate a new curriculum targeted at middle school students that would be implemented by D.A.R.E. instructors.

Working with Sloboda, D.A.R.E. agreed to a few changes to its model. First, D.A.R.E. would focus on an older cohort of students because many researchers believed it was important to supplement the educational services provided to fifth and sixth graders with a "booster shot" delivered to students a few years later. Second, D.A.R.E. agreed to revise their curriculum to make it less didactic and more participatory. Instead of "just say no" lectures about drugs, the police officers involved would attempt to engage youth people in conversations about the consequences of illegal drug use.

Emboldened by the endorsement of the Robert Wood Johnson Foundation, D.A.R.E. America launched an ambitious plan to revise its core program. In 2000, every D.A.R.E. instructor across the country was retrained and the curriculum revamped. Gone was the old style of one-way lectures by police officers. In its place was a new model in which officers led students in role-playing exercises and discussion groups. Officials at D.A.R.E. America sought to recast D.A.R.E. as an educational program that taught kids about how to make better decisions about drug use and a range of other issues. As a chastened Glenn Levant told the *New York Times* in 2001, "There's quite a bit we can do to make it better and we realize it." In a statement that must have stunned many close observers, Levant added, "I'm not saying it was effective, but it was state of the art when we launched it. Now it's time for science to improve upon what we're doing."[6] The banner headline on D.A.R.E. America's web site said it all: "It's a New D.A.R.E."

## Good Reasons for Ignoring Good Evaluation

The kind of criticism that D.A.R.E. received from scholars and the national media should have been enough to kill the program. Yet to this day, D.A.R.E. is alive and well.

This puzzled Carol Weiss, a professor at Harvard University's School of Education. So she set out to answer the riddle of how a program could remain popular in the face of overwhelming and well-publicized evidence of failure. Her first instinct was to conclude that local communities were either uninformed or were ignoring the research. "I initially thought it was because practitioners were not paying attention," she said (Weiss 2008).

Weiss's specialty is examining the impact of research on government decisionmaking. As Weiss writes, until the 1960s, evaluation research was not used routinely in the way we understand it today. While social reformers in the late 19th and first half of the 20th century conducted surveys and employed other research methods to document the extent of problems like poverty, they rarely took the time to evaluate the effectiveness of their responses to these problems because they assumed what they were doing was intrinsically good (Weiss 1998b). Only in the mid-1930s did foundations first start devoting funding to program evaluation, in an effort to bring a tough-minded skepticism to social policy. At times, this meant identifying some programs as failures after they initially had been deemed successful. For example, the landmark study of the Cambridge-Somerville youth worker program, famous for breaking new ground in scientific rigor, found that the program had no effect on juvenile or adult arrest rates among 506 delinquent youth over a 30-year period (Dishion, McCord, and Poulin 1999).

For the past 50 years, evaluation research has carried the threat of bad news. One response is for policymakers to ignore the research. Weiss's first brush with that reality came after the release of a study she conducted of a community service project based in Harlem that was funded as part of the War on Poverty. Her report was greeted with deafening silence. "I had the feeling I could have just dumped it into the ocean and it would have made no difference," Weiss said. "So, I asked myself: 'Why did they support and fund this evaluation if they were not going to pay any attention to it?' That's how I got interested in the uses of research" (Graff and Christou 2001).

Weiss initially believed that research on D.A.R.E. was being treated like her Harlem study. A true scientist, Weiss decided to test her assumption by sending a team of graduate students to interview educators, local politicians, and police officers in 16 school districts in four states (Colorado, Massachusetts, Kentucky, and Illinois) to assess the effects that research on D.A.R.E. had on the field (Birkeland, Murphy-Graham, and Weiss 2005).

Of the 16 school districts in the study, eight were using D.A.R.E. at the time the study began in 2001 and eight were not.

The team quickly learned that, far from ignoring the evidence about D.A.R.E., officials in the 16 school districts were well aware of it. "When we got into the field, we found out they were paying attention," remarked Weiss (2008). While few had taken the time to read the lengthy reports written by Dennis Rosenbaum and others, almost without exception they had seen or read something about them. Some had even cut out negative stories about D.A.R.E. from newspapers, which they shared with Weiss's interviewers. As a result, they were familiar with the broad outlines of the critique of D.A.R.E. Damage had been done: six communities had discontinued D.A.R.E. only a few years before the study started, and two additional communities dropped it by the time Weiss's team conducted follow-up interviews in 2003.

In each case, negative research findings played a role in the decision to drop D.A.R.E. One example was the Gardner, Illinois, school district, which discontinued the program in 1998 after the district's health coordinator saw a critical magazine article about D.A.R.E. that her husband had saved for her.[7] She convinced the school district to drop D.A.R.E. in favor of another drug prevention program. In Marlboro, Kentucky, the city manager and a local police lieutenant jointly decided to discontinue D.A.R.E. after reading stories in the newspaper that confirmed their personal beliefs that the program was ineffective. They also arranged for a D.A.R.E. critic from the University of Kentucky to address the local board of commissioners, who later voted to end the program. In Orchard Grove, Massachusetts, a local gadfly used negative evaluation findings to convince the town's governing board to end the program over the objections of the school superintendent, a strong D.A.R.E. supporter (Weiss 2005).

Another important factor for local communities that dropped D.A.R.E. was the perception that the federal government did not approve of the program. In 2002, the Department of Education issued a list of 9 "exemplary" and 33 "promising" youth drug prevention programs that were eligible for federal funding. D.A.R.E. did not make either of the lists, which were released in a preliminary document in 1998 and then embedded in federal legislation passed in 2002, over D.A.R.E. America's vigorous objections (Weiss 2005). Although this provision did not explicitly prohibit local school districts from using D.A.R.E., in practice many officials interpreted it as doing so. For example, in Cartersville, Colorado, which had a popular D.A.R.E. program in operation for 10 years (D.A.R.E. officers were known in Cartersville as "minor local celebrities"), school officials reluctantly dropped the program because they believed the federal government had left them with no choice (Birkeland et al. 2005).

As these examples show, D.A.R.E. did not emerge from its battle with researchers unscathed. Negative research findings clearly damaged the program's reputation. But a question remained: why had some communities in Weiss's study kept D.A.R.E. in the face of the evidence and the federal government's inferred criticism of the program?

What Weiss and her team found was surprising. To be sure, some jurisdictions kept D.A.R.E. in response to vigorous lobbying from D.A.R.E. But this was not the case in all places. Far from blithely ignoring or dismissing the research out of hand, local decisionmakers in many communities gave relatively sophisticated reasons for retaining D.A.R.E. One reason commonly cited was that local officials were realistic about what D.A.R.E. could do to combat illegal drug use. For example, a school board member in Massachusetts told interviewers that she thought it was "silly" to expect that D.A.R.E. alone would lower rates of drug use among young people. This perspective inoculated officials against some of the outlandish claims made by D.A.R.E. spokespeople—and against some of the harshest attacks by D.A.R.E. critics.

Local officials thought scholars had erred by focusing almost exclusively on the program's official goal of reducing drug use. Instead, they cited a number of secondary reasons to support the program, starting with the positive relationships it fostered among police officers, students, and educators. As one Massachusetts school superintendent put it, "If you ask . . . [whether it] reduces the illegal use of drugs and alcohol, apparently D.A.R.E. can't demonstrate that for various reasons. If you ask . . . [whether] it helps kids understand their community better . . . [or if] it produces favorable relationships between police and kids, all of the survey results . . . [are] positive" (Birkeland et al. 2005, 252). After helping a student with a difficult family situation, one police officer in Kentucky remarked that his interaction was almost impossible to capture in a study. "[It's] not something that you put on a bar graph or a pie chart or anything like that," he said (Birkeland et al. 2005).

Weiss's research team uncovered several examples of ancillary benefits of D.A.R.E. For example, D.A.R.E. officers at one Colorado high school helped reassure students that it was safe to reenter their school after the shootings at nearby Columbine High School. The benefits appeared to flow in both directions: a number of police officers interviewed said that participating in D.A.R.E. helped improve their image of young people, because they had a chance to interact with them in a nonadversarial setting. Many police officers, like Frank Kolarik, also enjoyed their work with D.A.R.E., so the program had a positive impact on job satisfaction. And police chiefs valued the relationships the program fostered with school officials. "One of the most important benefits and by-products is the relationship we have now with the school department," said one Massachusetts police chief. "It couldn't be better . . . it really couldn't be better. If I need anything, I just have to pick up the phone" (Birkeland et al. 2005, 252).

Barbara Topoil, the principal of Wampus Elementary where Frank Kolarik teaches D.A.R.E., echoes many of the observations made by Carol Weiss and her graduate students. "I know that D.A.R.E. has gotten a bad rap in terms of whether it truly prevents children from using drugs," she said. "I'm not sure [researchers] are asking the right questions. There are a lot of positives for our students who interact with Frank, and I don't know how you measure that" (Topoil 2008).

In many jurisdictions, school administrators ended up valuing their personal experience with D.A.R.E. more than they did the scholarly research. Many study informants told Weiss's research team that they believed their local D.A.R.E. program was better than other D.A.R.E. programs and thus qualified as an exception to the rule. On the one hand, it's possible that these local officials were merely displaying examples of the so-called "Lake Wobegon" effect, named for Garrison Keillor's satirical observation that in his fictitious hometown, "all the women are strong, all the men are good-looking, and all the children are above average." Yet, as researchers often point out, while good evaluation research can help provide probabilities about whether a program generally works or not, it does not foreclose the possibility that a particular version can be effective. "I have to say, I had a little bit of a crisis of faith during the study after hearing so many people say, 'our town is different,' " said Sarah Birkeland, one of Weiss's graduate students who worked on the study. "Generalizability is an idea that we researchers take for granted, but I realized that I hadn't thought about it all that deeply" (Birkeland 2008).

Many supporters of D.A.R.E. can point to personal experiences that convinced them of the value of the program. As Kathleen Vellenga, a Minnesota state legislator, put it:

I became a fan of D.A.R.E. when I was asked to be a presenter at an elementary [school] D.A.R.E. graduation. The room was packed with parents. The principal informed me this was the first time many of the parents had shown up at the school for any event. Many of the children were bused from the high poverty areas into this economically stable school neighborhood. As I drove back to my office, I recognized one of the fathers about a half mile from the school, trudging in the hot sun toward the bus stop that would take him back to his neighborhood. As I continued to attend D.A.R.E. events, I found that there seemed to be a pattern of bringing parents to their child's school. This is no small achievement. In the end, I decided to keep supporting the program, not because it proved to reduce substance abuse, but because it had other benefits. (Vellenga 2008)

Always quick to coin a phrase, Weiss writes that communities continued with D.A.R.E. in the face of negative research findings out of a combination of "rationality and rationalization." As she and her coauthors conclude in their well-titled paper, "Good reasons for ignoring good evaluation," local officials were far from ignorant pawns in the hands of the D.A.R.E. America propaganda machine. "Their decisions to continue implementing [D.A.R.E.]," they write, "are based on an assessment of the pros and cons, rather than simple ignorance" (Birkeland et al. 2005, 254).

## Deciding What Works and What Doesn't

It would be comforting to imagine a world in which failure was clearly and decisively identified by objective scholars and ineffective programs were shut down as a result. If more than thirty high-quality studies have reported a consistent finding that D.A.R.E. has no long-term impact on youth drug use, isn't the appropriate response, in the words of Dennis Rosenbaum, to "just say no to D.A.R.E."?

Yet as Weiss's study shows, the D.A.R.E. story is more complicated than it first appears. Far from being ignorant of the research, local decision-makers weighed the evidence about D.A.R.E. in deciding whether to keep the program. In many communities, the result was that D.A.R.E. was discontinued. In places where D.A.R.E. was retained, the decision was sometimes politically motivated. But not always. Many educators and elected officials ended up valuing the ancillary benefits of D.A.R.E., such as improved relationships with the police. These hard-to-measure, qualitative benefits are the most likely explanation for why D.A.R.E. remains in place in 75 percent of school districts across the country.

The limited impact of D.A.R.E. research should not come as a surprise, as it conforms to the basic pattern observed in so-called "knowledge utilization" studies of the past thirty years. As Carol Weiss and others have shown, evaluation research rarely has a direct effect on policymakers. While research can at times help challenge conventional wisdom, more often than not it is used to justify preconceived beliefs and decisions. "If practitioners are in favor of some action and they find an evaluation doesn't show positive effects, they tend to disregard it or make up excuses," said Weiss. "On the other hand, if they're against the program or the policy, and the study shows it wasn't effective, they are apt to champion the findings" (Weiss 2008).

Ultimately, there is no single objective standard for determining whether a program works. This seems particularly true in the case of D.A.R.E. While noting that local jurisdictions have articulated a number of reasons for keeping D.A.R.E., Dennis Rosenbaum flatly rules them out on the grounds that D.A.R.E. America had already committed itself to achieving a single goal. "Although I appreciate these 'voices,' " he writes, "I must add that D.A.R.E. was marketed and sold exclusively for its drug prevention benefits, not for other possible outcomes" (Rosenbaum 2007, 820).

To be sure, the scholarly critiques of D.A.R.E. have made an enormous contribution to the field, forcing D.A.R.E. America to improve its curriculum and injecting a healthy dose of skepticism into the youth drug prevention debate. However, neither D.A.R.E. America nor D.A.R.E. critics like Rosenbaum have the exclusive authority to set the terms by which a program like D.A.R.E. is judged. What the D.A.R.E. story shows is the importance of maintaining a dynamic balance among *all* of the key stakeholders involved in formulating criminal justice policy—academics, criminal justice officials, the public, the media, and politicians. If we had listened exclusively to the researchers who wanted to shutter D.A.R.E., we would have missed a host of ancillary benefits that the program has provided to local communities. Of course, if we had listened exclusively to the staff at D.A.R.E. America, we would have continued to unthinkingly replicate a model that failed to achieve its primary objective.

In the past decade, there have been dozens of articles written about D.A.R.E. Almost without exception, they tell a similar story: how D.A.R.E. America has bamboozled educators and the public into supporting a failing program.[8] The real story is that, in the case of D.A.R.E., local practitioners got it mostly right. They were able to sift through the completing claims of researchers and D.A.R.E. America and make somewhat reasoned judgments about whether to keep D.A.R.E. Their message to D.A.R.E., broadly speaking, contained equal parts warning and support. They were willing to stick with D.A.R.E., but only if it changed how it operated.

## The Limits of Research

Unfortunately for D.A.R.E. America, the effort to rebrand D.A.R.E. ("It's a New D.A.R.E.") has had mixed results. With funding from the Robert Wood Johnson Foundation, Zili Sloboda at the University of Akron designed an ambitious new curriculum, titled "Take Back Your Life," targeted to 9,500 seventh and ninth graders in Detroit, Houston, Los Angeles, New Orleans, Newark, and St. Louis. The curriculum focused on a smaller set of topics and allowed for more back-and-forth conversation between students and D.A.R.E. instructors.[9]

While early results released in late 2002 were encouraging, events outside Sloboda's control complicated her research design. Hurricane Katrina was a double blow: many of the students who fled New Orleans moved to Houston, creating problems halfway through the research process at two of the six research sites.[10] An even more critical problem was that Sloboda realized that her control group had been contaminated. Under ideal circumstances, the control group would receive no drug prevention education at all, which would allow for a better test of the effectiveness of D.A.R.E. However, "most kids get some kind of drug prevention education these days," said Sloboda. "And that is good news for our kids, but a big challenge to researchers" (Sloboda 2008).[11]

After seven years and considerable expense, officials at D.A.R.E. America are pessimistic about what the research will tell them. "I'm not sure anyone is ready to rigorously test any substance abuse curriculum in a real world environment," said D.A.R.E. America Executive Director Frank Pegueros, noting the problems experienced by Sloboda. "Zili found out that the complexities of large-scale research are such that it takes on a life of its own and you lose control of it" (Pegueros 2008). Officials at D.A.R.E. America acknowledge that one major goal of Sloboda's work, which was to shift the focus of D.A.R.E. to older students in middle school who are more at risk of drug abuse, has failed to come to fruition—the overwhelming majority of D.A.R.E. instructors still work at the elementary school level.

The D.A.R.E. story provides ample evidence of both the benefits and limits of research. Even the highest-quality and best-funded research does not provide easy answers. Rarely does research provide simple thumbs-up or thumbs-down judgments. For many policymakers, the only question they want answered is whether a given program works or not. Of course, reality usually is more complicated than that. Many programs work for *some* participants *some* of the time. In fact, Weiss believes that the best researchers can hope for is to enlighten policymakers about the problems they face and their policy options, rather than dictate decisionmaking. "Evaluation is not a substitute for judgment," she says (Weiss 2008).

While the fight over D.A.R.E. is mostly over, the controversy exposed a gap between researchers and practitioners that continues to this day. Some degree of conflict between these two worlds probably is inevitable. Social scientists and criminal justice officials have different value systems and divergent worldviews—often they are separated by training, location, professional rewards, and even the vocabulary they use (Fox 2004).

Despite the obstacles, criminal justice researchers and practitioners find themselves in a codependent relationship. Many practitioners are desperate for a more reflective approach to criminal justice that uses both qualitative and quantitative data to identify problems and assess solutions. Similarly, many researchers are eager to have their work taken more seriously and to have a broader impact on policy decisions.

The D.A.R.E. story offers a number of important lessons about the research-practice divide, including the challenges of implementing rigorous experimental studies, assessing all of the potential impacts of a multifaceted program, and creating an honest and civil dialogue between researchers and the administrators of an evaluated program.

The last lesson is perhaps the most important. The conflict between D.A.R.E. administrators and researchers reached a fever pitch because so much was at stake for the participants: D.A.R.E. felt it was fighting for its very life and the researchers felt they were fighting for their professional integrity (Rosenbaum 2007). But it didn't have to be that way. If the culture of criminal justice policymaking in this country were different, the D.A.R.E. story might have unfolded with much less acrimony. Is it possible to create a culture that values both reflection and results? That supports research but understands its limitations? That sets high expectations for practitioners but acknowledges the intransigent nature of many of the problems they are trying to solve? That understands that it is impossible to have trial without error?

Ultimately, the future of D.A.R.E. hinges on hundreds of separate judgment calls being made at the local level. How these decisions get made depends on a range of factors, including research results, local politics, the personal predilections of key decisionmakers, and, increasingly, fiscal realities. For state governments and police departments that are looking to cut budgets in the midst of an economic downturn, D.A.R.E. may end up being a tempting target. For example, New York State in 2008 dropped its D.A.R.E. funding, which included $150,000 for officer training, workbooks, and a full-time state D.A.R.E. coordinator.[12] New York City, which used to have 100 D.A.R.E. officers, no longer operates the program.

For his part, Frank Kolarik believes that the negative attention received by D.A.R.E. has had a dramatic impact. "In many regards, the D.A.R.E. brand is tarnished," he says. In 2008, at the request of D.A.R.E. America, Kolarik agreed to step in as the New York State D.A.R.E. coordinator on a voluntary basis, but says he's "not sure where the money will come from" to pay for the annual two-week officer training sessions of new D.A.R.E. instructors (Kolarik 2008).

The news is not all bad for D.A.R.E. however. For years, a fierce debate raged over the appropriateness of police officers as instructors, particularly in low-income communities where relationships with the police are historically poor. However, when Sloboda and her colleagues surveyed over 6,000 students in her target cities, she found that students gave higher ratings to police instructors than to other instructors (Hammond et al. 2008).[13]

This finding would not surprise the students, administrators, and teachers at Wampus Elementary. Nor would it surprise Frank Kolarik. "Some of the best cops I know are D.A.R.E. officers," Kolarik says. After 12 years in the trenches of D.A.R.E., however, Kolarik knows there always will be some people who will never be convinced of D.A.R.E.'s effectiveness. "What I've learned," Kolarik says, "is that where you stand is where you see" (Kolarik 2008).

# Conclusion

In 2004, journalist Michael Lewis wrote a book about the "quest for the secret of success in baseball" (Lewis 2004). *Moneyball* told the story of Oakland Athletics (A's) general manager Billy Beane, who, with limited financial resources, established a remarkable record for finding undervalued baseball talent and defeating more well-financed opponents.

When Lewis wrote *Moneyball,* the A's were in the midst of an eight-year stretch in which they didn't have a single losing season. During this run, they made the playoffs five times. From 1999 through 2005, the A's won an average of 94 games per year with an average annual payroll of $42 million. By contrast, the most successful and richest team of the era, the New York Yankees, averaged just three more wins each year while spending $98 million more *per season.*

As *Moneyball* details, the A's accomplished this remarkable record using some unconventional methods, including a reliance on statistical analysis to buttress traditional baseball scouting techniques. Based in no small part on the success of the book, Billy Beane was widely hailed as a visionary. He received numerous awards. He was named baseball's executive of the year. His approach to talent evaluation was emulated by a plethora of teams desperate to achieve maximal results with minimal payout. He became a sought-after speaker not just at sporting events but at business conferences. He even penned an op-ed for the *New York Times* with Newt Gingrich and John Kerry about how to use his data-driven approach to solve the health care crisis.

If Billy Beane's tenure as general manager had ended in 2006, the narrative arc of his professional life would have been a straightforward one: underdog achieves success, reaps the rewards, and then teaches others how to follow his example.

But Billy Beane did not leave baseball in 2006. And the years since then have not been particularly kind to his reputation. The A's have fallen back to earth, suffering through three consecutive losing seasons. Similarly, the record of Beane's selections in the 2002 amateur draft, which is the subject of an entire chapter in *Moneyball*, has been something less than earthshaking. In the book, the A's are overjoyed with their picks, which include "two of the three best right-handed pitchers in the country, and two of the four best position players" (Lewis 2004, 115). Unfortunately, not one of these players has gone on to become a star, and several are already out of baseball.

The point here is not to denigrate Billy Beane—his record as an executive is a strong one, all things considered. But the Billy Beane story does highlight one of the most important lessons of our book: anyone who claims to know the secret of success should be viewed with a dose of skepticism. There are no magic wands when it comes to achieving difficult goals. This is true in baseball. This is true in business. And this is certainly true in criminal justice.

No one can say with any degree of precision why the crime rate goes up or down. New York City's drop in crime since the early 1990s is arguably the most important criminal justice story of the past generation. Given its significance, one would assume that there would be a definitive analysis of what happened in New York and why. But scholars have been arguing for years about how best to explain the New York "miracle," with no resolution in sight (Kelling 2009).

We wish we could tell you how to reduce crime. We wish we knew how to guarantee that criminal justice reform efforts will succeed. But we don't. For those readers looking for foolproof recipes or Svengali figures to follow, this book will no doubt be a disappointment.

Instead of describing what works, we have spent the past six chapters highlighting the many different ways that attempts to reform the criminal justice system can go wrong. The criminal justice system is predicated on failure of course. The whole system is designed to go into action when things go wrong, when someone breaks the law. But that's not the kind of failure that this book is about. Nor is this book a critique of the structural failings of the criminal justice system. With the possible exception of our health care infrastructure, no institution has been labeled "broken" more often than the criminal justice system. The critiques come from all angles. Whether the focus is race (the disproportionate representation of minority groups), economics (the exorbitant cost of incarceration), fairness (the lack of a level playing field between the defense bar and the prosecution), morality (the continued use of the death penalty), or simple effectiveness (high recidivism rates), it is possible to argue that the entire criminal justice apparatus—from police investigation to prosecution to adjudication to incarceration to release—is a failure.

But we are not making that argument. Rather, this book has sought to examine what we would call "promising failures"—efforts to improve the criminal justice system that have achieved something less than unqualified successes. In truth, the only kind of success possible in the field of criminal justice is a qualified one; even the best, most well-implemented initiatives are incapable of producing entirely crime-free communities. In writing this book, we have found failure in the midst of success: for example, efforts to replicate successful models like drug court and Operation Ceasefire that did not achieve lasting results. We also have found elements of success amid failure: for example, the D.A.R.E. program, which has been deemed a failure by researchers but has achieved some significant victories along the way.

In the preceding pages, we have attempted to tell the stories of committed reformers in a broad range of professions—judges, cops, attorneys, parole officers, researchers, educators, and politicians who, despite their talent and ambition, nonetheless failed to achieve their goals. Through the lens of their experiences, and our own, we have identified a number of failure traps that reformers stumble into repeatedly. What follows are some of the most common mistakes that reformers have made over the past 25 years, along with some thoughts about how to address these problems in the future.

**Mistake 1: Failing to engage in self-reflection.** President Barack Obama, speaking about education reform, has said, "One of the things we want to get out of is this notion that somehow one law, one program, magically is going to change things. What happens then is people get disappointed, they scrap it, and they try a whole new thing."[2] This dynamic should be instantly recognizable to anyone who has worked in the field of criminal justice. Criminal justice is not immune to faddishness. As in sports, academia, business, and the arts, criminologists are always on the lookout for the "next big thing." One of the forces that fuels faddishness is the fact that self-analysis is not always a treasured value in the often macho, get-things-done, paramilitary world of criminal justice. Of the four types of failure that we identified when looking at the St. Louis Consent to Search program, the failure to engage in self-reflection is perhaps the most difficult to remedy. There are numerous obstacles that stand in the way of reformers engaging in meaningful self-analysis, including discomfort or unfamiliarity with research methodology and a natural tendency to engage in cheerleading in order to protect new ideas from external attack.

**Lesson: Criminal justice officials should constantly ask themselves what's working, what isn't, and why.** Self-examination is vital to the long-term health not just of reform efforts but of the entire criminal justice field. Unfortunately, as we saw in the chapter on parole reform in California, when budgets shrink, it is enormously tempting for government agencies to abandon luxuries like research and development. Criminal justice officials would in fact be wise to go in the other direction, bolstering their analytical capacity so they are better able to make policy arguments grounded in hard data and to make midcourse adjustments to flagging initiatives. An ongoing commitment to research and analysis can help reduce the likelihood that today's innovation becomes tomorrow's conventional wisdom in need of being overturned.

**Mistake 2: Defining success too narrowly.** Reducing crime should be the central goal of the criminal justice system. However, contrary to what many politicians seem to think, this is not the only goal that matters. In addition to reducing crime, the projects we have profiled in this book tried to achieve a broad range of other objectives, including solving the underlying problems of defendants, improving perceptions of fairness, reducing the use of incarceration, enhancing public trust in justice, and eliminating conflict and inefficiency among criminal justice agencies. Unfortunately, these types of goals often are more difficult to measure than whether the crime rate goes up or down.

**Lesson: Reducing crime is just one of many outcomes that should be sought from the criminal justice system.** Criminal justice officials must aggressively seek to educate both elected officials and the general public about the myriad goals of criminal justice reform. Only then can accurate report cards be developed for measuring criminal justice experiments instead of the pass-fail approach that is so prevalent today. This book is, in part, an effort to promote a more nuanced understanding of criminal justice innovation. Instead of just asking "does this program work or not?" reformers should be posing a different set of questions:

- What makes a program work in one place but not in another?
- Is it possible to identify successful elements within unsuccessful programs?
- Does a given initiative work better for some populations than for others?

A more sophisticated analysis of criminal justice will provide answers to questions like these and help the field create interventions that truly target the problems they seek to solve.

**Mistake 3: Thinking that more research will lead to purely rational, evidence-based criminal justice policies.** Is there a need for more criminal justice research in this country? Absolutely. The decline in federal spending devoted to criminal justice research in recent years should be a national concern.[3] Is it important for criminal justice innovators to be able to document their impacts with hard data rather than simply relying on feel-good anecdotes? For sure. But it would be a mistake to think that simply funding more research will lead to the crafting of purely rational, evidence-based criminal justice policies. We saw in the case of Operation Ceasefire that researchers have had a hard time saying for certain whether the initiative was responsible for Boston's remarkable success in improving its murder rate. And we saw in the chapter on D.A.R.E. that evaluators do not always take into account the ancillary benefits of a multifaceted initiative. While research can tell us a lot, very few evaluations offer the types of simple, categorical judgments about what works and what doesn't that policymakers crave.

**Lesson: Evaluation is no substitute for judgment.** Going forward, stronger bridges between research and practice need to be built. Policymakers and practitioners must become better consumers of social science research. They must learn to distinguish between rigorous and shoddy evaluations. And they must understand that caveats and conditional judgments often are the best that can be expected from researchers. On the other side, researchers must do a better job of explaining the differences among various research methodologies. In particular, they must take pains to explain the value not just of randomized trials (the gold standard of social science) but quasi-experimental studies, process evaluations, focus groups, neighborhood surveys, structured interviews, and other forms of information gathering. They must be more willing to venture educated guesses even in the face of incomplete information. They must acknowledge that while research should play a bigger role in decisionmaking than it has up until now, it is just one of many factors that go into formulating criminal justice policy. At the end of the day, as Harvard professor Carol Weiss says, "Evaluation is no substitute for judgment."

**Mistake 4: Expecting too much from criminal justice reform efforts.** According to Paul Gary Wyckoff, author of *Policy and Evidence in a Partisan Age,*

> Government policy is consistently oversold, to citizens, to politicians, and even to academics. It is oversold by both conservatives and liberals, in different but curiously similar ways. Over and over, we elect officials in the naïve belief that they can pull some magic lever to fix our social and economic problems. When that doesn't work, we "throw the bums out" and elect someone else to pull a different lever or to pull the same lever in the opposite direction. But what many Americans don't understand, but empirical studies bear out, is that in many circumstances the governmental levers are simply disconnected from the problems they are supposed to address. (Wyckoff 2009, 3–4)

Although Wyckoff is writing about economics, education, and social policy, he just as easily could be describing the world of criminal justice. In general, policymakers and the public need to have realistic expectations of how much the criminal justice system can achieve. David Wilson, a professor at George Mason University, observes, "Most criminal justice interventions only work with people for a short period of time. For example, a court-mandated batterer intervention typically only involves about 28 contact hours. Changing behavior that has developed over a lifetime in 28 hours is a tall order" (Wilson 2008).

**Lesson: Our expectations of criminal justice reform should be modest.** Given the limitations of time and resources, it is remarkable that any criminal justice intervention is able to change the behavior of offenders. The truth is that the individuals involved in the criminal justice system bring a staggering array of problems with them, including joblessness, addiction, mental illness, and low literacy levels, as well as histories of poverty and abuse. Helping these individuals to get on the right track and avoid criminal behavior is no easy job. This is a difficult message to deliver to the public, and to political officials. But having a more honest conversation about criminal justice reform means redefining expectations. "Realistic expectations are important," says researcher Carol Weiss. "With criminal justice programs, it's hard, slow work. It's a little odd that people expect so much from them. When you run an advertising campaign for Toyota, changing sales by a percentage point or a two is considered a huge success. The same is true in running a big election campaign. Why is that different in criminal justice?" (Weiss 2008).

**Mistake 5: Failing to navigate local politics.** In our first chapter, we saw how an innovative gun recovery program in St. Louis that achieved early success failed to develop a plan for long-term support inside the police department. As a result, the project was abandoned soon after the appointment of a new police chief. This is not an isolated phenomenon. It is enormously tempting for new leaders to jettison the ideas and initiatives associated with their predecessors. Most innovations require government support or endorsement at some level, so criminal justice reformers constantly must grapple with the political realities of elected officials and high-ranking bureaucrats. Government leaders often demand simple solutions and quick fixes, not to mention public credit. These factors tend to undermine innovation and even can lead to the implementation of politically appealing programs (such as boot camps or gun-buyback programs) without a strong evidence base. But politics is not always a bad thing, of course, as the chapter on Connecticut's response to the Cheshire tragedy makes clear. Political pressure is often the only force capable of overcoming bureaucratic inertia, mobilizing broad support for change, and keeping well thought-out reform plans from being prematurely abandoned.

**Lesson: It is amazing what can be accomplished when you don't care about who gets the credit.** What is the coin of the realm in public policy? Unlike in business, it isn't money—it's public acknowledgment. People are attracted to new ideas for a host of reasons. For some, the motivation is idealism, a desire to make the world a better place. For others, the motivation may be less lofty—many see reform efforts as a way to make a name for themselves and advance their careers. While the quest for public recognition can help generate momentum for reform, it can also be a destructive force. The unraveling of Operation Ceasefire in Boston offers a vivid example of how the fight for credit can undermine an initiative. It may be a cliché, but reformers would do well to remember the old Harry Truman line that it is amazing how much you can accomplish when it doesn't matter who gets the credit. Figuring out how to provide key political actors with the credit they need (be it applause at a public event, a favorable story in the local paper, or a trip to a national conference)—regardless of whether they deserve it or not—is a crucial skill for reformers to master.

**Mistake 6: Planning in isolation.** In an increasingly heterogeneous world, it is difficult for criminal agencies to achieve meaningful results when they act in isolation. Unfortunately, the criminal justice system rarely functions as a coherent system: it is more like the National Basketball Association—a set of independently operated teams locked in an eternal struggle against each other. Given the conflicting agendas and cultures among the various criminal justice agencies, it is a challenge to get the police, probation, parole, corrections, prosecution, courts, defense bar, and pretrial service agencies to line up behind any single idea. As a result, there is a tendency for criminal justice agencies to go it alone, limiting the planning of new initiatives to a small cadre of internal players. This is a mistake. As we have seen in cases like Consent to Search, if the circle of people involved in a new initiative is too small, the project may have a hard time generating support once the initiators move on, as they inevitably will.

**Lesson: Collaboration should be approached strategically.** Of course, many reformers err in the other direction as well, laboring under the impression that if they could just get everyone around the table, they would be able to hammer out a consensus on a course of action. According to Ron Corbett, the executive director of the Massachusetts Supreme Court, "In my 33 years, I've never seen real change come about from getting everyone at the table. Every time you add another big agency to your planning effort, the difficulty of getting people to agree and to coordinate goes up geometrically. As a result, you are doomed before you start" (Berman 2008, 106). As is often the case, the most prudent approach is something in between these poles. Reformers need to be strategic in deciding how and when to bring relevant stakeholders to the table—both under- and over-inclusiveness can have potentially devastating long-term consequences.

**Mistake 7: Not spending enough time on the details of implementation.** While it is crucial to have good ideas, the truth is that most criminal justice experiments fail for other reasons—good ideas are relatively plentiful. Far more difficult is mastering the challenges of implementation. It isn't enough to simply identify best practices and then disseminate them to the world. The case studies in this book offer vivid evidence of how implementation problems, both big and small, can derail even the most well-conceived programs.

**Lesson: Context matters.** There's basically no such thing as an idea or program that can be taken off the shelf and successfully implemented regardless of conditions on the ground. Gary Hinzman who oversees correctional services in Cedar Rapids, Iowa, calls this the "copycat" problem:

> I've seen this across the country, where a jurisdiction tries to copy a successful program without really thinking it through or having regard for proper implementation. In Iowa, for example, we created a computerized risk assessment tool that took two to three years to develop. A lot of people in other states have asked to have us to send them the program on a computer disc, but I always tell them I'm reluctant to do so. Our tool reflects a lot of judgment calls that the director of a corrections agency has to be comfortable living with. As a former police chief, it's hard for me to be painted as soft on crime, so I was willing to take some risks. And then there are issues like the availability of treatment resources, availability of sanctions, and programming, which differ from state to state. In the end, each department must develop a tool like this that is custom designed for their use. (Hinzman 2008)

There are no cookie-cutter models when it comes to criminal justice innovation. The same program that works well in Miami (drug court) can struggle in Minneapolis and Denver. The same ideas that reduce crime in Boston (Operation Ceasefire) can fail to catch on in Los Angeles. Instead of seeking foolproof formulas, it should be acknowledged that every place is different and there are hundreds of different ways to achieve success.

**Mistake 8: Taking a top-down approach to change.** The chapter on parole reform in California highlighted a key tension that criminal justice reformers almost inevitably confront: to make things happen, you need political approval from the top ranks of government, but the ultimate success or failure of any effort will depend on implementation on the ground by front-line staff—probation officers, judges, police officers, and others. An exclusively top-down approach to reform, in which change is simply dictated from above, can lead to resentment or even outright sabotage by line staff. As Robert Keating, who served as the criminal justice coordinator for New York under Mayor Ed Koch, concludes, "Often the best ideas fail because we have not gotten a buy-in from the people that do the work. In the past, some great ideas have died a stillborn death because line staff would hear about them and say one of two things: (A) 'We don't think that is a great idea, so we're not going to do it,' or, (B), 'We know [that] if we stall, there will be another commissioner and he will have a whole new set of ideas' " (Berman 2008, 107).

**Lesson: The people at the bottom of an agency matter as much as the people at the top.** It is difficult to achieve positive results without belief—

the people charged with implementation must have some faith that what they are being asked to do makes sense. However, it is next to impossible to believe in a reform that you have played no role in conceiving. As a result, reformers, particularly those who are not line staff, must take pains to market their ideas across all levels of an agency's hierarchy. They also must take care to leave room for some invention at the ground level, allowing line staff to tweak and embroider a program to suit their needs. The good news is that reformers can reap significant rewards if they pursue this course of action—often the most effective way of spreading an idea is by generating positive word of mouth among those who have been directly involved in successful implementation efforts.

\* \* \*

The one overarching lesson that we have learned over the course of writing this book is that there is no such thing as a guarantee of success. Reform efforts, even those that have achieved good results in other settings, fail as often as they succeed. Moreover, the criminal justice system is remarkably impervious to reform. There are many who argue that no matter how much you poke it, twist it, or massage it, the system has the ability to return to its original shape (Berman 2008).

William Goldman, the author of dozens of successful screenplays (including *Butch Cassidy and the Sundance Kid*), once wrote: "Nobody knows anything... nobody—not now, not ever—knows the least goddam thing about what is or isn't going to work at the box office" (Goldman 1989, 41). In our darker, more nihilistic moments, we are sometimes tempted to apply Goldman's skepticism about Hollywood to the field of criminal justice and declare that nobody knows anything about how to reduce crime. But we wrote this book because we think it is in fact possible to advance the state of knowledge in the field and for the criminal justice system to continue to get smarter and more effective.

While we are cautiously optimistic about the potential for reform within the criminal justice system, we also believe that meaningful change will not happen by simply promulgating successful initiatives. Our decision to celebrate failure is a deliberate one. By analyzing a series of projects that failed to meet expectations, we have sought to accomplish two goals. First, we hope to provide useful lessons to the innovators of tomorrow, helping them avoid the mistakes of their predecessors. Just as important, we hope to encourage future risk-taking by nudging the field of criminal justice away from a culture of finger-pointing that scorns those who deviate from orthodoxy when they fall short of their ambitions.

While our research has not unearthed a foolproof path to successful reform, we do know how to guarantee failure, and that is to continue with business as usual—cycling the same individuals through the criminal justice system again and again, spending billions of dollars unnecessarily on prisons, and tolerating public disenchantment with justice. This book is dedicated to all those who have the courage, fortitude, and creativity to risk failure and challenge the status quo in the criminal justice system.

# Afterword
*Greg Berman*

When Aubrey Fox and I published *Trial & Error in Criminal Justice Reform: Learning from Failure* in 2010, we knew we were not writing for a mass audience. At the time, criminal justice reform was a topic of interest only to a narrow band of practitioners and advocates who toiled away diligently but largely anonymously.

As the old English song goes, the world has turned upside down since then.

Ferguson happened. Baltimore exploded. Eric Garner and Kalief Browder became household names. Black Lives Matter shifted the terms of public debate. The *New York Times* made an editorial decision to focus on criminal justice issues. Right on Crime emerged as a powerful conservative voice on criminal justice policy. President Obama chose to devote a fair amount of political energy during his final term to criminal justice, including a high-profile visit to a federal prison—the first-ever such visit by a sitting president. A bipartisan movement emerged on Capitol Hill to advance the idea of changing overly-punitive federal sentencing laws.

It is safe to say that, today, criminal justice reform is a topic of urgent, national interest. Editorial writers, politicians, foundation executives, and other influential voices have begun to ask a set of hard questions: How do we reduce the use of incarceration? Are there ways to address the disproportionate impact that the justice system has on the lives of young black and Latino men? What can be done to restore public trust in justice in low-income neighborhoods and among communities of color? And how do we do all of this while continuing to reduce crime and improve public safety?

The answers to these questions are the subject of intense conversation from state to state and city to city. But what is not open to debate is the fact that the status quo within the justice system is not working and that significant change is required. Across a fairly broad political spectrum, there is a consensus that the time for criminal justice reform is now.

How long this current moment will last is anyone's guess. Given the realities of a fast-changing world and short political attention spans, the safe bet is that the window of opportunity will not be open for long.

Even as we attempt to seize the current moment by devising new reforms and launching new initiatives, it is crucial that we look backward to learn from the mistakes of the past. That is why Aubrey Fox and I wrote this book.

*Trial & Error in Criminal Justice Reform* is built around a series of case studies. In each chapter, we examine a criminal justice program that, despite the best efforts of decent, hard-working, and competent reformers, failed to achieve its desired impact. Some of these initiatives, like the St. Louis Consent to Search program, are no longer in operation.

But many of the programs that we discuss in *Trial & Error in Criminal Justice Reform* are still with us. Indeed, some are at the very center of the criminal justice reform agenda in this country.

For example, in chapter 3, we examine the complicated legacy of Operation Ceasefire, a violence reduction initiative that achieved spectacular results in Boston before disintegrating in acrimony. While Operation Ceasefire is no more, one of the founders of the program, David Kennedy, has gone on to become one of the most influential criminal justice thinkers in the country. In the years since we wrote *Trial & Error in Criminal Justice Reform*, Kennedy has launched a new organization (the National Network for Safe Communities) that has won multiple grants from the U.S. Department of Justice and encouraged dozens of localities to adopt the Operation Ceasefire model (albeit under a different name and with some modifications).

There are good reasons why the federal government and local municipalities have chosen to invest in Kennedy's ideas. A review of the evaluation literature sponsored by the Campbell Collaboration found that Kennedy's brand of "focused deterrence" has achieved significant reductions in offending in multiple locations. (See Anthony A. Braga and David L. Weisburd, "The Effects of 'Pulling Levers' Focused Deterrence Strategies on Crime," March 2012, The Campbell Collaboration.)

What we offer in *Trial & Error in Criminal Justice Reform* is a valuable companion to this research. It is not meant as a critique of Kennedy's model—indeed, I think highly of Kennedy's ideas. In recent years, my agency has worked to implement some of the basic elements of Kennedy's model in Brownsville, Brooklyn, in an effort to combat gun violence.

The chapter in *Trial & Error* devoted to Operation Ceasefire tells an important story about how difficult it is to bring the justice system and community groups together to tackle even the most pressing crime problems. It also highlights a key problem for criminal justice reformers: things tend to fall apart over time. As hard as it is to raise the money and generate the political will to launch a new program, it may be even more challenging to sustain good work over the course of months and years.

This lesson also applies to drug court, the alternative-to-incarceration program for addicted offenders that is the subject of chapter 2.

In the years since 2010, the research literature on drug court has become even more persuasive than it was when we wrote *Trial & Error*. A 2012 meta-analysis offered this straightforward conclusion: "the evidence indicates that adult drug courts reduce recidivism." (See Ojmarrh Mitchell, David B. Wilson, Amy Eggers, and Doris L. MacKenzie, "Assessing the Effectiveness of Drug Courts on Recidivism: A Meta-Analytic Review of Traditional and Non-Traditional Drug Courts," *Journal of Criminal Justice* 40 [2012]: 60–71.)

Bolstered by this kind of evidence—and federal grant funding—drug courts have continued to proliferate. According to the U.S. Department of Justice, as of 2014, the estimated number of drug courts operating in the United States was over 3,400. In recent years, both liberal and conservative politicians have sought to create more drug courts and expand the number of defendants who participate in these programs.

In general, I am a supporter of the drug court model—my agency helped to create New York City's first drug court in Brooklyn twenty years ago and we continue to provide technical assistance to drug courts across the country.

But in *Trial & Error in Criminal Justice Reform*, Aubrey and I describe the foibles of the drug courts in Denver and Minneapolis in some detail. In doing so, we sought not to discredit the model but to underline the challenges of getting implementation right. Just because a program is a success in one location does not mean it will succeed everywhere. We also sought to focus attention on the importance of leadership. The struggles in Denver and Minneapolis had a lot to do with succession planning, as the chief advocates for the drug courts moved on to other assignments.

The drug court and Operation Ceasefire case studies speak to the basic message underlying the entire book: change is hard. This is true when you have sufficient money, good ideas, talented people, and political buy-in. If you don't have one or more of these things, the odds against you increase exponentially.

It is more important than ever that we be honest about the difficulty of reforming the justice system. More eyes than ever are examining how our state and local justice systems operate. Thanks to their efforts, we have successfully diagnosed a broad range of problems, including the overreliance on cash bail, the misuse of incarceration, and the continued erosion of public confidence in justice among communities of color.

Persistent problems like these will not yield easily. It is going to take a sustained commitment of time, energy, and money over the course of many years to reform our justice system. Our goal in writing *Trial & Error in Criminal Justice Reform* was to prepare reformers for the long fight.

## After-Afterword

*Aubrey Fox*

A few years after the publication of our book, Greg and I had a meeting with a well-known English politician and he made a remark that has stuck with me: "We tend to overestimate the impact of our work in the short term and underestimate it in the long term."

As I reflect back on the writing of *Trial & Error in Criminal Justice Reform: Learning from Failure*, that quote holds unexpected resonance. One of the key lessons of the book (which is highlighted in Cy Vance Jr.'s splendid foreword) is that honesty compels us to have realistic expectations about what we as reformers can accomplish in the short term.

This theme is repeated throughout the case studies examined in our study, including the struggles experienced by the Denver and Minneapolis drug courts, the difficulties in sustaining successful approaches to urban violence in Boston and St. Louis, and California's struggles in managing its exploding prison population.

Fast forward to today, and the picture looks very similar, with reformers seeking to make incremental improvements while managing difficult problems. In 2014, St. Louis's homicide rate was the highest in the country (though it should be said that the surrounding metropolitan region is much safer). California's state prison population has dropped, but at least until this year, most of that decrease was offset by increases in the number of people held in county jails. At the same time, the Denver and Minneapolis drug courts are still in business. Taken together, does this add up to a picture of success or failure? Clearly it's a complicated answer.

If you take a step back, you can see that there are some profound changes taking place in the field of criminal justice. According to a report released by the Brennan Center for Justice, the national crime rate was cut in half from 1980 to 2013. In New York, that decline was 68 percent. New York is also remarkable in that it has simultaneously achieved steep reductions in incarceration.

How do we account for these dramatic improvements? Again, modest expectations are in order regarding our ability to ascribe causality. For example, the Brennan Center report examines no fewer than fourteen separate theories. (See Oliver Roeder, Lauren-Brooke Eisen, and Julia Bowling, "What Caused the Crime Decline?" February 2015, Brennan Center for Justice.)

While it may be reassuring to assume that long-term change always moves in a positive direction, that is clearly not the case. For even as we are experiencing broad and sustained crime drops, we are also dealing with some very serious questions about how the criminal justice system relates to regular citizens (particularly citizens of color), questions that this country has struggled with since its founding.

For a would-be criminal justice reformer reading this book, I would offer two pieces of advice. The first is that I would not be discouraged by the challenges of accomplishing even incremental change in the short term. Quite the contrary. In fact, one of the things that Greg and

I hoped to accomplish was to make the minutiae of policy implementation as interesting in its own way as the bigger picture issues that tend to get written about.

It turns out that much of the real craft of criminal justice reform can be found in the small adjustments reformers make every day in response to the unique context and challenges they face. Beyond their particular details, the stories told in our case studies are meant to honor a set of criminal justice reformers who sought to tackle issues like drug addiction, urban violence, and mass incarceration despite facing long odds.

A second piece of advice is to keep in mind the conundrum raised in my opening paragraph—that as bad as we tend to be about predicting the impacts of our actions in the short term, we tend to be even worse in the long run. This echoes important recent insights from social psychologists such as Phillip Tetlock, who has written that our ability to predict change more than five years into the future is extremely limited. (See Phillip Tetlock and Dan Gardner, *Superforecasting: The Art and Science of Prediction*, Crown Publishing, 2015.)

This view of the world makes me more of an optimist than a pessimist. For while we may not be able to predict the impact of our actions, we should always remember that our day-to-day efforts might lead, eventually, to profoundly positive change.

# Notes

## Introduction

1. Our point is not to disparage such books. Indeed, we helped write a book that explicitly seeks to sell a new idea (Berman and Feinblatt 2005).

2. While criminal justice has a lot to learn from fields like medicine, it should be noted that there are good reasons a more scientific approach does not prevail in criminal justice, including the logistical, ethical, and financial obstacles to conducting randomized trials on a routine basis.

3. Thomas M. Burton, "Flop Factor: By Learning from Failures, Lilly Keeps Drug Pipeline Full," *New York Times,* April 21, 2004, p. A1.

4. Billy Bragg, "North Sea Bubble," *Don't Try This at Home.* Lyrics available at http://www.lyrics007.com/Bragg%20Billy%20Lyrics/North%20Sea%20Bubble%20Lyrics.html.

5. In 1974, sociologist Robert Martinson and several coauthors published a meta-analysis of the evaluations from various rehabilitation programs; Martinson then wrote a widely read essay on the topic in *The Public Interest* (Martinson 1974). The conclusion was that there was no appreciable evidence of the programs' impact on recidivism. While many scholars have subsequently debunked this research, the idea that "nothing works" to change the behavior of offenders had a lasting impact, helping to discredit the idea of rehabilitation. Similarly, the urban problems of the 1970s and 1980s led many to conclude that American cities like New York were "ungovernable" (Cannato 2001).

6. The commercial can be found on YouTube at http://www.youtube.com/watch?v=m-EMOb3ATJ0.

## Chapter 1. The Four Types of Failure

1. The account in this chapter is largely based on two reports written by these two researchers for the United States Department of Justice (Decker and Rosenfeld 2001, 2004).

2. See *Washington Post*, "Gun Search Program to Be by Request Only: D.C. Backs Off from Door-to-Door Outreach," April 4, 2008. See also *Boston Globe*, "Police Set to Search for Guns at Homes: Voluntary Program Is Issue in Community," February 9, 2008; ard *Philadelphia Inquirer*, "Nutter Defiantly Signs Five Gun Laws," April 12, 2009.

3. "We should have announced this with a lot more information," Chief Cathy L. Lanier told the *Washington Times*. "I take full responsibility for not announcing this with more information." *Washington Times*, "D.C. Chief Clarifies Gun Search Program," April 3, 2008. The program ran for only a few months as part of a "summer of safety" initiative announced by the Chief.

4. According to Richard Rosenfeld, as a metropolitan area, and not just a city, St. Louis actually ranks a comfortable 120th in crime. *USA Today*, "Why City Crime Rankings Offer a Misleading Picture," November 29, 2007. While Rosenfeld is undoubtedly correct in saying that St. Louis is safe for 87 percent of its residents, it remains quite dangerous for some populations. For example, 43 of the 59 murder victims in the first five months of 2008 were black men. *St. Louis American*, "St. Louis Murder Rate May Shoot Past Last Year's Total," May 27, 2008.

## Chapter 2. Failure amid Success

1. Bureau of Justice Statistics, *Drug and Crime Facts*, http://www.ojp.usdoj.gov/bjs/dcf/tables/arrtot.htm.

2. *New York Times*, "Nice City's Nasty Distinction: Murders Soar in Minneapolis," June 30, 1996.

3. *Denver Westword News*, "A Chemistry Experiment: The Denver Drug Court Tests a Formula for Reclaiming Addicts," September 26, 2002.

4. *Rocky Mountain News*, "Panel Pushing to Revive Part of City's Drug Court," April 14, 2006.

5. Although both drug courts have been revived in recent years, they are much smaller and no longer have the boundless ambition outlined by their founders. *Minnesota Public Radio*, "Courting Changes in Drug Prosecution," November 29, 2006.

6. *New York Times*, "Miami Tries Treatment, Not Jail, in Drug Cases," February 19, 1993.

7. *New York Times*, "Miami Tries Treatment."

8. *New York Times*, "Miami Tries Treatment."

9. *Denver Westword News*, "A Chemistry Experiment."

10. *Denver Westword News*, "A Chemistry Experiment."

11. *Denver Post*, "Profile: Bill Ritter—Former DA Follows Own Path," July 31, 2006.

12. To be fair, this dynamic was not unique to drug court: judges in Minnesota were long in the habit of "departing" from sentencing guidelines set by the state and from sentencing recommendations made by prosecutors.

13. *Minneapolis Star-Tribune,* "Two Big Problems Are the Root Causes of Rising Crime," June 15, 2006.

14. *Minnesota Public Radio,* "Courting Changes."

15. *New York Times,* "Innovative Courts Give Some Addicts Chance to Straighten Out," October 15, 2008.

16. *New York Times,* "Innovative Courts."

17. *USA Today,* "Our View on Crime and Punishment: Therapy with Teeth," October 21, 2008.

# Chapter 3. The Complicated Legacy of Operation Ceasefire

1. *New York Times,* "In Boston, Nothing Is Something," November 21, 1996.

2. *Christian Science Monitor,* "What's at the Root of Boston's Rise in Murders?" May 10, 2006.

3. Suzanne Smalley, "New Commissioner Focuses on Gun Crimes," *Boston Globe,* December 4, 2006.

4. Teny Gross, "Politics, Petty Feuds, and Street Violence," *Boston Globe,* February 12, 2006.

5. The other inspiration for Project Safe Neighborhoods was a more traditional law enforcement program based in Richmond, known as Project Exile.

6. Alex Kotlowitz, "Blocking the Transmission of Violence," *The New York Times Magazine,* May 4, 2008.

# Chapter 4. The Billion-Dollar Failure

1. *New York Times,* "New Tact on Straying Parolees Offers a Hand Instead of Cuffs," May 17, 2008.

2. *North County Times,* "Revolving Doors: The Crisis in California's Parole System," November 23, 2008.

3. *Sacramento Bee,* "California Is Toughest State on Parolees," November 21, 2008.

4. *Los Angeles Times,* "Brown Calls Sentencing Law a Failure," February 28, 2003.

5. "Governor Schwarzenegger Appoints Secretary and Staff of the Department of Corrections and Rehabilitation," press release, Office of the Governor, July 1, 2005.

6. *Washington Post,* "California's Crisis in Prison Systems a Threat to Public," June 11, 2006.

7. *Washington Post,* "California's Crisis."

8. *Sacramento Bee,* "California Prison Package Hailed," May 4, 2007.

9. *Sacramento Bee,* "Deal Stalls on California Prisons," September 25, 2008.

10. *Orange County Register,* "Orange County Would Test Shorter Parole Terms for Non-Violent Criminals," September 18, 2007.

11. Joan Petersilia, "Parole, the Right Way," *Los Angeles Times,* October 8, 2007.

12. *Orange County Register,* "Orange County Would Test."

13. *Sacramento Bee,* "Deal Stalls."

14. *New York Times,* "California Asks Removal of Prisons Overseer," January 28, 2009.

15. *Associated Press,* "Prison System Receiver Stays," March 25, 2009.

16. *San Francisco Chronicle,* "No More Options in State Prisons' Future," August 2, 2009.

17. In their study of the Houston Intensive Supervision Parole (ISP) program in the mid-1980s, Susan Turner and Joan Petersilia followed 458 parolees assigned to ISP for a year. Compared to routine parolees, ISPers had more contact with their parole officers (6.5 contacts per month vs. 2.5 for the control group), were supervised by parole officers with smaller caseloads (25 to 1, compared to 85 to 1), had more access to services like drug treatment or family therapy (55 percent received services vs. 32 percent), and were drug-tested more often (84 percent vs. 9 percent). Yet the results were discouraging. There was no difference in reoffending. But ISPers in Houston averaged 2.2 technical violations, compared to 0.4 for routine parolees. In part, this was due to the frequency of drug testing: almost all ISPers were tested for drugs, and 70 percent tested positive as opposed to 3 percent of routine parolees. By the time the year was over, about 35 percent of ISPers were returned to prison, compared to 20 percent of routine parolees. When all supervision, court, and incarceration costs were factored in, ISPers in Houston "cost" $6,788 on average in 1998 dollars, as opposed to $3,960 for routine parolees (Turner and Petersilia 1992).

18. *New York Times,* "California Officials Fear Abduction Case May Hurt Efforts on Parole," August 30, 2009.

19. As of September 2009, the bill is awaiting the signature of Governor Schwarzenegger. *Christian Science Monitor,* "Dugard Case: Is California's Parole System Overstretched?" September 2, 2009.

20. *New York Times,* "Report Faults Parole System in Abduction," November 4, 2009.

# Chapter 5. Beyond Simple Solutions

1. To cite one example, in the late 1990s and early 2000s, the state of Washington passed five bills into law bearing the names of victims, including the "Becca Bill," the "Teekah Lewis Act," "Anton's Law," the "Dane Rempfer Bill," and the "Joey Levick Bill." Jim Bruner, "Crime Laws Bear Names of Young Victims." *Seattle Times,* March 31, 2000.

2. Some have suggested that Three Strikes actually makes some violent criminals even *more* violent. According to Radha Iyengar of Harvard University, the probability that third-strike-eligible offenders would commit a more violent crime increased by 9 percent. The likely explanation is that offenders understood that a more violent offense would be treated no differently than any other third-strike-eligible crime (Iyengar 2007).

3. Katie Melone, "State's Prison Population Not Expected to Increase," *Hartford Courant,* February 15, 2007.

4. *New York Times,* "Neighbors of Home Invasion Victims Demand Stricter Repeat-Offender Laws," August 19, 2007.

5. *New York Times,* "Rell Reveals Plan to Improve Parole System," January 13, 2008.

6. *New York Times,* "An Effort to Integrate Crime Data Gets a Chief," November 9, 2008.

7. *New York Times,* "Connecticut Halts Parole for Crimes of Violence," September 23, 2007.

8. *New York Times,* "Plan to Transfer More Inmates Draws Criticism in Connecticut," August 1, 2003.

9. Melone, "State's Prison Population."

10. Melone, "State's Prison Population."

11. *Waterbury Republican-American,* "Governor Against $260 Million Proposal to Build Two Prisons," November 10, 2007.

12. *New York Times,* "An Effort to Integrate Crime Data."

13. Connecticut Senate Democrats, "Democratic Senate Passes Tougher Persistent Offender Bill, Allocates $10 Million for Criminal Justice," press release from Connecticut Senate President Pro Tempore Donald Williams and Senate Majority Leader Martin Looney, April 23, 2008. Available at http://www.senatedems.ct.gov/pr/leaders-080424.html.

14. Christine Stuart, "Three Strikes Coalition Revives the Debate," *CTNews-Junkie,* September 28, 2008. Available at http://www.ctnewsjunkie.com/legal/three_strikes_coalition_revive.php.

15. Christine Stuart, "A Referendum on Three Strikes?" *Connecticut News Junkie,* November 7, 2008.

16. *New Haven Register,* "It Was a Tough Day to Be a Republican in Connecticut," November 5, 2008.

# Chapter 6. Defining Failure

1. This chapter builds upon the authors' previously published analysis of D.A.R.E. (Berman and Fox 2009).

2. D.A.R.E. America points to a study by Dennis M. Gorman and J. Charles Huber, Jr., and another by Carol H. Weiss in arguing that the D.A.R.E. program has been held to a standard higher than have other youth drug prevention programs. For example, as Gorman and Huber have written, "What differentiates D.A.R.E. from many of the programs on evidence-based lists might not be the actual intervention but rather the manner in which data analysis is conducted, reported, and interpreted." However, none of the authors suggest that D.A.R.E. is an effective intervention, as measured by reductions in illegal drug use among young people (Gorman and Huber 2009; Weiss 2008).

3. *USA Today,* "Studies Find Drug Program Not Effective," October 1, 1993.

4. *USA Today,* "Studies Find."

5. *Seattle Post-Intelligencer,* "Stamper Wants to Cut D.A.R.E., 17 Positions," June 17, 1996. Stamper also criticized D.A.R.E. in an interview with *PBS NewsHour with Jim Lehrer* on April 25, 1997.

6. *New York Times,* "Anti-Drug Program Says It Will Adopt a New Strategy," February 1, 2001.

7. The school districts that participated in the study were given fictional names.

8. See Elliot (1995). See also Jennifer Gonnerman, "Truth or D.A.R.E.: The Dubious Drug-Education Program Takes New York," *Village Voice,* April 7, 1999; and Jodi Upton, "D.A.R.E.: Failing Our Kids," *Detroit News,* February 27, 2000. The most notorious example of an anti-D.A.R.E. piece was an article written by Stephen Glass, who was later revealed to have fabricated a number of his articles; the piece attracted a $50 million lawsuit from D.A.R.E. America and was eventually settled out of court (see Glass 1997).

9. Carnavale Associates, "Study Highlights Value of D.A.R.E. Network," press release.

10. Students who participated in the new program showed small but statistically significant improvements in terms of their attitudes toward drugs and their drug refusal skills. "It shows us that the program is doing what it intended to do, and in a very significant way," Sloboda told a reporter from Associated Press. Of course, the key question was whether the results would hold true over the long haul, or if the benefits of D.A.R.E. would dissipate over time as they had in previous studies. Associated Press, "Schools D.A.R.E. to Get Real," October 29, 2002.

11. For their part, D.A.R.E. critics like Dennis Rosenbaum believe that these are not valid excuses, particularly given the study's large sample size and the reality that all youth drug prevention research faces the same challenge of potential control group contamination.

12. *Daily Messenger,* "State Drops Funding for D.A.R.E. Program," June 17, 2008.

13. In addition, in recent years D.A.R.E. America has demonstrated its continuing willingness to rethink its approach to substance abuse prevention. In 2007, D.A.R.E. America reached an agreement with Pennsylvania State University to use "keepin' it REAL" as its new middle school curriculum. The curriculum is listed on the Substance Abuse and Mental Health Services Administration's National Registry of Evidence-Based Programs and Practices. See http://www.nrepp.samhsa.gov/programfulldetails.asp?program_id=119.

# Conclusion

1. *Washington Post,* "President Obama Discusses New 'Race to the Top' Program," July 23, 2009.

2. Alfred Blumstein, a prominent criminologist at Carnegie Mellon University, says that "the National Institutes of Health spends $400 million a year on dental research. The National Institute of Justice spends $50 million a year on criminal justice research." *New York Times,* "The Real Murder Mystery? It's the Low Crime Rate," August 2, 2009.

# References

American Bar Association, Division of Public Education. 2008. "The Independence of the Judiciary." *Law Day 2008 Speech Ideas/Talking Points.* http://www.abanet.org/publiced/lawday/talking/judicialelections.html.

Baez, Gail. 2008. Interview.

Barnette, Toddrick. 2008. Interview, October 22.

Belenko, Steve. 2001. "Research on Drug Courts: A Critical Review, 2001 Update." New York: National Center on Addiction and Substance Abuse at Columbia University.

Berman, Greg, ed. 2008. "Learning from Failure: A Roundtable on Criminal Justice Innovation." *Journal of Court Innovation* 1(1): 97–121.

Berman, Greg, and John Feinblatt. 2005. *Good Courts: The Case for Problem-Solving Justice.* New York: New Press.

Berman, Greg, and Aubrey Fox. 2002. "Going to Scale: A Conversation about the Future of Drug Courts." *Court Review* 39(3): 4–13.

———. 2008. "Embracing Failure: Lessons for Court Managers." *The Court Manager* 23(4): 20–26.

———. 2009. *Lessons from the Battle over D.A.R.E.: The Complicated Relationship between Research and Practice.* New York: Center for Court Innovation.

Bhati, Avinash Singh, John K. Roman, and Aaron Chalfin. 2008. "To Treat or Not to Treat: Evidence on the Prospects of Expanding Treatment to Drug-Involved Offenders." Washington, DC: The Urban Institute.

Birkeland, Sarah. 2008. Interview, July 1.

Birkeland, Sarah, Erin Murphy-Graham, and Carol Weiss. 2005. "Good Reasons for Ignoring Good Evaluation: The Case of the Drug Abuse Resistance Education (D.A.R.E.) Program." *Evaluation and Program Planning* 28(3): 247–56.

Boyle, Patrick. 2001. "A DAREing Rescue: How an Intervention by Critics and Federal Officials Brought the Youth Anti-drug Program into Rehab." *Youth Today,* April 1.

Braga, Anthony A. 2008. "Pulling Levers: Focused Deterrence Strategies and the Prevention of Gun Homicide." *Journal of Criminal Justice* 36(4): 332–43.

Braga, Anthony A., David Hureau, and Christopher Winship. 2008. "Losing Faith? Police, Black Churches, and the Resurgence of Youth Violence in Boston." *Ohio State Journal of Criminal Law* 6(1): 141–72.

Braga, Anthony A., David M. Kennedy, Annie M. Piehl, and Elin J. Waring. 2001. "Part II. Measuring the Impact of Operation Ceasefire." In *Reducing Gun Violence: The Boston Gun Project's Operation Ceasefire.* NIJ Reducing Gun Violence Series Research Report NCJ 188741. Washington, DC: National Institute of Justice.

Brickner, Adam. 2008. Interview, October 8.

Burke, Kevin. 2008. Interview, September 24.

Burlingame, Michael. 2008. *Abraham Lincoln: A Life.* Baltimore, MD: Johns Hopkins University Press.

Cannato, Vincent. 2001. *The Ungovernable City: John Lindsay's New York and the Crisis of Liberalism.* New York: Basic Books.

Clear, Todd. 2008. Interview, September 4.

Connecticut Office of Policy and Management, Criminal Justice Policy and Planning Division. 2009. *2009 Connecticut Correctional Population Forecast Report: A Report to the Governor and Legislature.* http://www.ct.gov/opm/lib/opm/cjppd/cjresearch/populationforecast/20090215_forecastingfinal.pdf.

Coppolo, George. 2008. "Parole during the 1980s." OLR Research Report 2008-R-0126. Hartford: Connecticut General Assembly, Office of Legislative Research. http://www.cga.ct.gov/2008/rpt/2008-R-0126.htm.

Cullen, Frank. 2008. Interview, September 16.

Decker, Scott H. 2008. Interview, May 22.

Decker, Scott H., and Richard Rosenfeld. 2001. *From Problem Solving to Crime Suppression to Community Mobilization: An Evaluation of the St. Louis Consent-to-Search Program.* NIJ Report NCJ 188291. Washington, DC: National Institute of Justice. http://www.ncjrs.gov/pdffiles1/nij/grants/188291.pdf.

———. 2004. *Reducing Gun Violence: The St. Louis Consent-to-Search Program.* NIJ Reducing Gun Violence Series Research Report NCJ 191332. Washington, DC: National Institute of Justice. http://www.ojp.usdoj.gov/nij/pubs-sum/191332.htm.

Dishion, Thomas J., Joan McCord, and Francois Poulin. 1999. "When Interventions Harm: Peer Groups and Problem Behavior." *American Psychologist* 54(9): 755–64.

Domanick, Joe. 2004. *Cruel Justice: Three Strikes and the Politics of Crime in America's Golden State.* Berkeley: University of California Press.

Duane, Daniel. 2006. "Straight Outta Boston." *Mother Jones* (January/February).

Elliot, Jeff. 1995. "Drug Prevention Placebo—How D.A.R.E. Wastes Time, Money, and Police." *Reason* 26:14–21.

Ericson, Rebecca, Sarah Welter, and Thomas L. Johnson. 1999. "Evaluation of the Hennepin County Drug Court." Minneapolis: Minnesota Citizens Council on Crime and Justice.

Farr, Bob. 2008. Interview, September 22.

Flesche, Miles. 2008. Interview, November 25.

Fox, Aubrey, ed. 2004. "Bridging the Gap: Researchers, Practitioners, and the Future of Drug Courts." Edited transcript of roundtable discussion. New York: Center for Court Innovation. http://www.courtinnovation.org/_uploads/documents/bridgingthegap.pdf.

Garcia, Charlie. 2008. Interview, September 29.

Glaser, Daniel. 1995. *Preparing Convicts for Law-Abiding Lives: The Pioneering Penology of Richard A. McGee.* Albany: State University of New York Press.

Glass, Stephen. 1997. "Don't You D.A.R.E." *Rolling Stone,* March 3.

Goldkamp, John S. 1994. "Miami's Treatment Court for Felony Defendants: Some Implications of Assessment Findings." *The Prison Journal* 73(2): 110–66.

———. 2003. "The Impact of Drug Courts." *Criminology* 2(2): 197–206.

Goldman, William. 1989. *Adventures in the Screen Trade: A Personal View of Hollywood and Screenwriting.* New York: Grand Central Publishing.

Gorman, Dennis M., and J. Charles Huber, Jr. 2009. "The Social Construction of 'Evidence-Based' Drug Prevention Programs: A Reanalysis of Data from the Drug Abuse Resistance Education (D.A.R.E.) Program." *Evaluation Review* 33(4): 396–414.

Graff, Fiona, and Miranda Christou. 2001. "In Evidence Lies Change: The Research of Whiting Professor Carol Weiss." *HGSE News,* September 10. http://www.gse.harvard.edu/news/features/weiss09102001.html.

Granfield, Robert, Cynthia Eby, and Thomas Brewster. 2002. "An Examination of the Denver Drug Court: The Impact of a Treatment-Oriented Drug-Offender System." *Law & Policy* 20(2): 183–202.

Grattet, Ryken, Joan Petersilia, and Jeffrey Lin. 2008. *Parole Violations and Revocations in California.* Research Report NCJ 224521. Washington, DC: National Institute of Justice. http://www.ncjrs.gov/app/Search/Abstracts.aspx?id=246487.

Gross, Teny. 2008. Interview, December 5.

Hammond, Augustine, Zili Sloboda, Peggy Tonkin, Richard Stephens, Brent Teasdale, Scott F. Grey, and Joseph Williams. 2008. "Do Adolescents Perceive Police Officers as Credible Instructors of Substance Abuse Prevention Programs?" *Health Education Research* 23(4): 682–96.

Heimberger, Bob. 2008. Interview, May 29.

Hewitt, Bill. 2007. "Horror in the Night." *People* 68(7): 4–5.

Hinzman, Gary. 2008. Interview, August 29.

Hoffman, Morris B. 2000. "The Drug Court Scandal." *North Carolina Law Review* 78(5): 1437–1527.

———. 2002. "The Denver Drug Court and Its Unintended Consequences." In *Drug Courts in Theory and in Practice,* edited by James L. Nolan, Jr. (67–87). New York: Aldine de Gruyter.

Hoffman, Tom. 2008. Interview, December 19.

Iyengar, Radha. 2007. "I'd Rather Be Hanged for a Sheep than a Lamb: The Unintended Consequences of 'Three-Strikes' Laws." Harvard Labor Economics Seminar presentation paper. Cambridge, MA: Harvard University.

Jacobson, Michael. 2006. *Downsizing Prisons: How to Reduce Crime and End Mass Incarceration*. New York: New York University Press.

———. 2010. Personal communication, May 6.

Jones, Van. 2008. *The Green Collar Economy: How One Solution Can Fix Our Two Biggest Problems*. New York: Harper.

Kane, Kevin. 2009. Interview, April 9.

Kelling, George L. 2009. "How New York Became Safe: The Full Story." *City Journal* 19 (special issue): 93–98.

Kennedy, David M. 1997. "Pulling Levers: Chronic Offenders, High-Crime Settings, and a Theory of Prevention." *Valparaiso University Law Review* 31(2): 449–84.

———. 2008. Interview, November 10.

Kennedy, David M., Anthony A. Braga, and Annie M. Piehl. 1997. "The (Un)Known Universe: Mapping Gangs and Gang Violence in Boston." In *Crime Mapping and Crime Prevention*, edited by David Weisburd and Tom McEwen (219–62). Monsey, NY: Criminal Justice Press.

———. 2001. "Part I. Developing and Implementing Operation Ceasefire." In *Reducing Gun Violence: The Boston Gun Project's Operation Ceasefire*. NIJ Reducing Gun Violence Series Research Report NCJ 188741. Washington, DC: National Institute of Justice.

Kolarik, Frank. 2008. Interview, October 15.

Kopp, Wendy. 2003. *One Day, All Children: The Unlikely Triumph of Teach for America and What I Learned along the Way*. New York: Public Affairs.

Kotlowitz, Alex. 2008. "Blocking the Transmission of Violence." *The New York Times Magazine*, May 4.

Larson, Gary. 2008. Interview, September 29.

Latessa, Ed. 2008. Interview, September 29.

Lawlor, Mike. 2009. Interview, January 29.

Leland, John. 1998. "Savior of the Streets—God vs. Gangs: What's the Hottest Idea in Crime Fighting? The Power of Religion." *Newsweek*, June 1.

Lewis, Michael. 2004. *Moneyball: The Art of Winning an Unfair Game*. New York: W.W. Norton & Company.

Little Hoover Commission. 2007. *Solving California's Corrections Crisis: Time Is Running Out*. Sacramento, State of California, Little Hoover Commission. Available at http://www.lhc.ca.gov/studies/185/report185.html.

Lipsky, Michael. 1980. *Street-Level Bureaucracy: Dilemmas of the Individual in Public Services*. New York: Russell Sage Foundation.

Long, Greg. 2008. Interview, October 7.

Martinson, Robert. 1974. "What Works? Questions and Answers about Prison Reform." *The Public Interest* 35 (Spring): 22–54.

McGarrell, Ed. 2008. Interview, October 7.

McGiveney, Jim. 2008. Interview, July 14.

McPhee, Michele. 2006. "Divine Wrath." *Boston Magazine* (December).

Merrill, Jeffrey C., Ilana Pinsky, Ley A. Killeya-Jones, Zili Sloboda, and Tracey Dilascio. 2006. "Substance Abuse Prevention Infrastructure: A Survey-Based Study of the Organizational Structure and Function of the D.A.R.E. Program." *Substance Abuse Treatment, Prevention, and Policy* 1:25.

Meyer, Bill. 2008. Interview, September 24.

Meyer, William G., and A. William Ritter. 2001. "Drug Courts Work." *Federal Sentencing Reporter* 14(3/4): 179–85.

Miller, Dennis. 2008. Interview, September 22.

Morgan, Helen. 2008. Interview, October 10.

Papachristos, Andrew. 2008. Interview, November 19.

Pegueros, Frank. 2008. Interview, June 26.

Petersilia, Joan. 2007. "Employ Behavioral Contracting for 'Earned Discharge' Parole." *Criminology and Public Policy* 6(4): 1501–9.

———. 2008. "Influencing Public Policy: An Embedded Criminologist Reflects on California Prison Reform." *Journal of Experimental Criminology* 4(4): 335–56.

Plotkin, Martha, ed. 1996. *Under Fire: Gun Buy Backs, Exchanges, and Amnesty Programs.* Police Executive Research Forum.

Przynski, Marie. 2008. Interview, October 8.

Ranum, Jane. 2008. Interview, September 24.

Rodriguez, Maritza. 2009. Interview, January 21.

Roehl, Jan, Dennis P. Rosenbaum, Sandra K. Costello, James R. Coldren, Jr., Amie M. Schuck, Laura Kunard, and David R. Forde. 2008. *Paving the Way for Project Safe Neighborhoods: SACSI in 10 U.S. Cities.* NIJ Research in Brief Report NCJ 216298. Washington, DC: National Institute of Justice.

Rosenbaum, Dennis P. 2007. "Just Say No to D.A.R.E." *Criminology & Public Policy* 6(4): 815–24.

———. 2008. Interview, June 13.

Rosenbaum, Dennis P., and Gordon S. Hanson. 1998. "Assessing the Effects of School-Based Drug Education: A Six-Year Multi-Level Analysis of Project D.A.R.E." *Journal of Research in Crime and Delinquency* 35(4): 381–412.

Rosenfeld, Richard. 2008. Interview, May 21.

Rosenfeld, Richard, Robert Fornango, and Eric Baumer. 2005. "Did Ceasefire, CompStat, and Exile Reduce Homicide?" *Criminology and Public Policy* 4(3): 419–49.

Sandoval, Raul. 2008. Interview.

Scott, Michael. 2008. Interview, May 14.

Simon, Jonathan. 2005. "Reversal of Fortune: The Resurgence of Individual Risk Assessment in Criminal Justice." *Annual Review of Law and Social Sciences* 1:397–421.

Skogan, Wesley G. 2008. "Why Reforms Fail." *Policing and Society* 18(1): 23–34.

Sloboda, Zili. 2008. Interview, June 23.

Smyth, Katya Fels, and Lisbeth B. Schorr. 2009. "A Lot to Lose: A Call to Rethink What Constitutes 'Evidence' in Finding Social Interventions That Work." Working Paper Series. Cambridge, MA: Harvard University, John F. Kennedy School of Government, Malcolm Weiner Center for Social Policy. http://www.hks.harvard.edu/centers/wiener/research-publications/working-papers.

Thompson, Mike. 2009. Interview, February 12.

Tita, George. 2008. Interview.

Tita, George E., K. Jack Riley, Greg Ridgeway, and Peter W. Greenwood. 2005. *Reducing Gun Violence: Operation Ceasefire in Los Angeles.* NIJ Reducing Gun Violence Series Research Report NCJ 192378. Washington, DC: National Institute of Justice.

Topoil, Barbara. 2008. Interview, October 8.

Travis, Jeremy. 2008. Interview, June 17.

Turner, Susan, and Joan Petersilia. 1992. "Focusing on High-Risk Parolees: An Experiment to Reduce Commitments to the Texas Department of Corrections." *Journal of Research in Crime and Delinquency* 29(1): 34–61.

Vellenga, Kathleen. 2008. Personal communication.

Warren, Jenifer. 2008. *One in 100: Behind Bars in America.* Washington, DC: Pew Center on the States. http://www.pewcenteronthestates.org/uploadedFiles/One%20in%20100.pdf.

Weisberg, Robert. 2005. "Meeting Consumer Demand in Modern Criminology." *Criminology & Public Policy* 4(3): 471–78.

Weiss, Carol H. 1998a. *Evaluation: Methods for Studying Programs and Policies,* 2nd ed. Upper Saddle River, NJ: Prentice Hall.

———. 1998b. "Have We Learned Anything New about the Use of Evaluation?" *American Journal of Evaluation* 19(1): 21–32.

———. 2008. Interview, June 27.

Weiss, Carol, Erin Murphy-Graham, and Sarah Birkeland. 2005. "An Alternate Route to Policy Influence: How Evaluations Affect D.A.R.E." *American Journal of Evaluation* 26(1): 12–30.

Wellford, Charles F., John V. Pepper, and Carol V. Petrie, eds. 2004. *Firearms and Violence: A Critical Review.* Washington, DC: National Academies Press.

Wieland, Lucy. 2008. Interview, October 22.

Wilson, David. 2008. Interview, June 11.

Winship, Christopher, and Jenny Berrien. 1999. "Boston Cops and Black Churches." *The Public Interest* 136 (Summer): 52–68.

Wyckoff, Paul G. 2009. *Policy and Evidence in a Partisan Age: The Great Disconnect.* Washington, DC: Urban Institute Press.

Yunus, Muhammad. 1999. *Banker to the Poor: Micro-Lending and the Battle against World Poverty.* New York: Public Affairs.

Zimring, Franklin E., Gordon Hawkins, and Sam Kamin. 2001. *Punishment and Democracy: Three Strikes and You're Out in California.* New York: Oxford University Press.

# Index

Adinolfi, Al, 92
African-American Churches in
    Dialogue, 18
American Bar Association (ABA), 39

Baca, Lee, 57
"backdoor sentencing," 64–65
Baez, Gail, 37
Barnette, Toddrick, 38, 39
Beane, Billy, 113–14
Berman, Greg, 7, 9, 120
Birkeland, Sarah, 107, 108
Board of Parole Hearings (BPH), 65
Boston, 45–46. *See also* Ceasefire,
    Operation
Boston Gun Project, 53. *See also*
    Ceasefire, Operation
Boston Ten Point Coalition, 54
Boyle, Patrick, 101
Braga, Anthony, 54–55
Brickner, Adam, 34, 35
Bronx Community Solutions, 4, 5
Brown, Jeffrey, 54
Burke, Kevin, 9, 27–28, 31, 36–38, 40,
    42, 43

Cahill, Peter, 43
California. *See also* parole in California;
    Three Strikes legislation
    problems in correctional system,
        63–65, 70
    transfer of authority for criminal
        justice policy to elected officials,
        68–69
California Correctional Peace Officers
    Association, 74
California Department of Corrections
    and Rehabilitation (CDCR), 72, 73
Caliguiri, Sam, 91, 92
Carruth, Keith, 71
Ceasefire, Operation, 17, 46–47, 58–60, 81
    as "Boston miracle," 46
    the Boston story, 45–50, 53–58, 60
    David Kennedy and, 46–48, 50, 51,
        53–56, 58, 59
    evaluating the effectiveness of, 57–58
    falling apart, 53–55
    "low point," 59
    Paul Joyce and, 47–48, 50, 51, 53, 55, 58
    ramifications, 60
    replicated in other cities, 55–60
    saving, 58–60
Center for Court Innovation, 4

Center for Evidence-Based Corrections, 72
Cheshire murders, 82–84, 86–89
  and postpartisan criminal justice,
    92–95
Clayton, Richard, 102
Clear, Todd, 81
Clinton, Bill, 46
collaboration, strategic approach
  to, 120
concept, failures of (bad ideas), 6, 21
Connecticut, 82–95. *See also* Cheshire
  murders; Lawlor, Mike
  reforming the system, 84–86
Connecticut Criminal Justice Information System, 90
Consent to Search program, 11–16,
  19–23, 81
  challenges faced and mistakes made,
    20–22
  iterations/phases of, 15–19, 21–22
  lessons learned from, 20
  a view from St. Louis, 24–25
"copycat" problem, 121
Corbett, Ron, 120
Coughlin, John, 34
criminal justice efforts, expecting too
  much from, 118–19
criminal justice officials
  communication with elected officials
    and the public, 70
  should ask themselves what's is and
    isn't working and why, 116
criminal justice reform. *See also specific*
  *topics*
  context of, 120–21
  expecting too much from, 118
  politics of, 39–42. *See also* politics
  top-down *vs.* bottom-up approach to,
    121–22
criminal justice reformers, common mistakes made by, 115–21
  lessons learned, 116–22
criminal justice system, outcomes sought
  by, 116–17
crises, legislation following. *See* Cheshire
  murders; tragic events
Cullen, Frank, 99

D.A.R.E. America, 97, 100–103, 108–10.
  *See also* Drug Abuse Resistance
  Education (D.A.R.E.) program
Decker, Scott, 12–19, 22–23
Denver. *See under* drug court
Determinate Sentencing Act of 1977, 68,
  70, 73
determinate sentencing structure, 84. *See*
  *also* "truth in sentencing" laws
Domanick, Joe, 79
Donner, Christine, 33
Dowd, Ed, 17
Drug Abuse Resistance Education
  (D.A.R.E.) program, 97–100
  Carol Weiss and, 104–9, 111, 118–19
  contentious relationship between
    scholarly community and, 100–103
  deciding what works and what doesn't
    work, 108–10
  Dennis Rosenbaum and, 99–102, 105,
    108, 109
  evaluations of effectiveness, 99–103
  good reasons for ignoring good
    evaluation, 103–8
  Frank Kolarik and, 97–100, 112
  and the limits of research, 110–12
drug arrests, 27–28
drug court, 28–39
  Bill Meyer and, 27, 28, 31–33, 35–36,
    40–43
  criticisms and unpopularity of, 37–38
  in Denver, 27–29, 31–36, 40–43
  evaluating the effectiveness of, 31, 39,
    42–43
  immediacy in drug treatment, 32–33
  Kevin Burke and, 27–28, 31, 36–38, 40,
    42, 43
  in Miami, 29–32
  in Minneapolis, 27–29, 31–33, 36–43
  overview, 28–31
  phases of treatment, 30
  and the politics of criminal justice
    reform, 39–42
  revolving door of, 37–38
drug treatment. *See* drug court
Duane, Daniel, 57
Dunford, Robert, 55

earned-discharge model, 73–74
evaluation. *See also* research, evaluation
    is no substitute for judgment, 117–18
Evans, Paul, 46, 55


faddishness, 115–16
failure(s), 1–3, 6, 9, 114–15
    causes of, 20–21
    is rarely black-and-white, 6–7
    types of, 6, 21
Farr, Bob, 83, 92–93
Federal Emergency Management Agency
    (FEMA), 81
Flesche, Miles, 41
Fox, Aubrey, 7, 9
Fox, James, 88
French, Gary, 45, 53, 55


gangs. *See* Ceasefire, Operation
Garcia, Charles, 34, 41
Garrido, Phillip, 78
Gates, Darryl, 100
Gelb, Adam, 86
Glaser, Daniel, 66–68
Goldkamp, John S., 30
Goldman, William, 122
Gross, Teny, 55, 56
gun buyback program, 12–13
gunlocks, 17
guns, 11, 19–20
    searching homes for, 11–15
    training for parents who own, 17


Hamilton, Alexander, 40
"hard cases make bad law," 80–82. *See
    also* Cheshire murders; tragic events
Hayes, Steven, 83
Heimberger, Bob, 17–19, 23–25
Hennepin County, 43
Hickman, Roderick, 71, 72
High Point Initiative, 59
Hinzman, Gary, 80, 121
Hoffman, Morris, 34, 35

Hoffman, Thomas, 70, 74
home release, supervised, 84–85
Hope, Education, Law, and Safety
    (HEALS), 55
Houston Intensive Supervision Parole
    (ISP), 128n.17


implementation
    failures of (poor execution), 6, 21
    spending enough time on the details
        of, 120–21
Intensive Supervision Parole (ISP),
    128n.17
International Ten Point Coalition, 54
Intervale Posse, 51–53
isolation
    planning in, 120
    projects operating in, 20


Jacobson, Michael, 64, 76
Joyce, Paul, 47–48, 50, 51, 53, 55, 58


Kane, Kevin, 89, 93, 94, 95
Keating, Robert, 121
Kelso, J. Clark, 74
Kennedy, David
    background and overview, 45
    Consent to Search program and, 17
    Operation Ceasefire and, 46–48, 50, 51,
        53–56, 58, 59
Kennedy, John F., 45
Kersten, Katherine, 37–38
Kings of Swamp Castle, 19
Klaas, Polly, 79
Klein, Herbert, 29
"knowledge utilization" studies, 108–9
Kolarik, Frank, 97–100, 112
Komisarjevsky, Joshua, 83, 86–88, 93


"Lake Wobegon" effect, 107
Larson, Gary, 43
Latessa, Ed, 39, 41

Lawlor, Mike, 81–82, 92
  changing the focus, 86–88
  confronting consequences, 88–90
  postpartisan criminal justice and, 93–95
  reforming the system, 84–86
  triumph, 90–91
Levant, Glenn, 100–103
Lewis, Michael, 113
Lipsky, Michael, 75
Long, Greg, 31–33, 35

Machado, Mike, 74
marketing, failures of, 6, 21
McCain, John, 42
McGarrell, Ed, 59
McGee, Richard, 66–71
McGiveney, Jim, 101–2
Meyer, Bill, 27, 28, 31–33, 35–36, 40–43
Miller, Dennis, 37, 38, 41–42
Minneapolis, Minnesota. *See under* drug
    court
Minnesota, 27–28
Mobile Reserve. *See* St. Louis Police
    Department Mobile Reserve Unit
Mock, Lois, 15–16
*Moneyball* (Lewis), 113, 114
Morgan, Helen, 41, 43

National Ten Point Coalition, 54
Night Light, Operation, 48, 54. *See also*
    Ceasefire, Operation

Obama, Barack, 1, 42, 115
Operation Ceasefire. *See* Ceasefire,
    Operation
Operation Night Light, 48. *See also*
    Ceasefire, Operation
O'Toole, Kathleen, 55

parole agents, accountability of, 75–76
parole in California, 61–65
  and the battle for reform, 66–68

  Joan Petersilia and, 66, 70–73, 78
  new era for parole reform, 74–76
  "new parole model," 72
  the politicization of crime and,
    68–70
  Raul Sandoval and, 61–62, 75–78
  Richard McGee and, 66–71
  two-track system for parolees, 78
  critique of, 64–65
parole of violent offenders in Connecti-
    cut, ban on, 82, 84–85, 91, 94
Parole Violation Decision Making Instru-
    ment (PVDMI), 62–63, 75–77, 81
Parolee Resource Center, 63
parolees "churning" in and out of prison
    for technical violations, 64
Pegueros, Frank, 110
Petersilia, Joan, 7, 66, 70–73, 78, 78,
    128n17
Petit, William, Jr., 82–83, 91. *See also*
    Cheshire murders
Petit-Chapman, Johanna, 91, 92
politicization of crime, 68–70
politics
  of criminal justice reform, 39–42
  failures of, 21
  impact on success or failure of
    reforms, 7, 14–15
  navigating local, 21, 119
"prison reentry" centers, 73
Project Safe Neighborhoods, 56
Przynski, Marie, 37
public, communication between criminal
    justice officials and researchers and
    the, 70
Public Safety and Offender Rehabilitation
    Services Act of 2007, 72–73
"pulling levers" strategy, 52, 54

Ranum, Jane, 37
Reagan, Ronald, 68
Red Hook Community Justice Center, 4–5
reform. *See* criminal justice reform
rehabilitation. *See* drug court
Rell, Jodi, 82, 84, 88–91, 94

Reno, Janet, 28
research, evaluation, 104, 117. *See also
under* Drug Abuse Resistance Education (D.A.R.E.) program
and rational, evidence-based criminal justice politics, 117–18
researchers, communication with elected officials and the public, 70
Reynold, Mike, 79
Richardson, Joseph, 11
Risk, Simon, 13, 15, 17, 18
risk taking, need for, 9
Ritter, Bill, 35, 36
Rivers, Eugene, 46, 47, 54
Robert Wood Johnson Foundation, 102–3
Rodriguez, Maritza, 75–76
Rosenbaum, Dennis P., 99–102, 101, 105, 108, 109
Rosenfeld, Richard, 12, 16, 19, 22–23, 57, 126n5
Rowland, John G., 82, 85
Ryan, Jessica, 83

Sandoval, Raul, 61–62, 75–78
scandal, setting crime policy in reaction to the latest, 92. *See also* tragic events
Schorr, Lisbeth, 8
Schrunk, Michael, 6
Schwarzenegger, Arnold, 66, 71, 72, 74
Scott, Michael, 2, 23, 54
self-reflection, failure to engage in, 6, 21, 22, 115–16
Skogan, Wesley, 41
Sloboda, Zili, 103, 110
Slutkin, Gary, 56
"Solving California's Correctional Crisis: Time Is Running Out," 63–64
St. Louis, 24–25. *See also* Consent to Search program
murder rate, 12–13
St. Louis Consent to Search program. *See* Consent to Search program
St. Louis Police Department Mobile Reserve Unit, 13–16
Stamper, Norm, 102

Stern, Donald, 52
Strategic Approaches to Community Safety Initiatives, 56
success, defined too narrowly, 116
supervised home release, 84–85

Ten Point Coalition, 48, 54
Thompson, Michael, 82, 84, 88, 93–94
Three Strikes legislation
in California, 79, 80, 82
in Connecticut, 82–84, 87–94
party politics and, 94
negative unintended consequences, 80, 128n.2
Tita, George, 56, 57
Topoil, Barbara, 98, 107
tragic events, outrage and legislation following, 80–82, 92, 93. *See also* Cheshire murders
Travis, Jeremy, 23
trial-and-error process, 2, 5, 24, 58
"truth in sentencing" laws, 68–69. *See also* determinate sentencing structure
Turner, Susan, 128n17

Vamp Hill Kings, 51–52
Vellenga, Kathleen, 107–8

Wallens Ridge prison, 85
War on Poverty, 104
Weisberg, Robert, 58
Weiss, Carol H., 104–9, 111, 118–19
Wieland, Lucy, 31–32, 38, 39
Williams, Donald E., Jr., 91
Wilson, David, 118
Wilson, Pete, 79
Wyckoff, Paul Gary, 118

Youth Violence Strike Force, 47, 48, 50, 51

"zero tolerance" policy for parole and probation violations, 82

# About the Authors

**Greg Berman** is the director of the Center for Court Innovation, a public-private partnership that seeks to reduce crime, aid victims, and improve public trust in justice. The Center has won numerous prizes for innovation, including the Peter F. Drucker Award for Nonprofit Innovation and the Innovations in American Government Award from the Ford Foundation and Harvard University. Greg is the coauthor (with John Feinblatt) of *Good Courts: The Case for Problem-Solving Justice* (The New Press).

**Aubrey Fox** is the director of special projects for the Center for Court Innovation, where he is responsible for a range of initiatives, including the Center's efforts to launch a new office in London. Prior to that, Aubrey was the project director of Bronx Community Solutions, a program that provides judges in the Bronx with alternative sanctions for misdemeanor cases.